HELP!
I'm Starting a
New Business

A Step by Step Guide in Starting a New Business

NATISCHA HARVEY

DISCLAIMER

<u>LIMIT OF LIABILITY/DISCLAIMER OF WARRANTY:</u>

While the author and publisher have used their best efforts in preparing this book, the author and publisher are not offering it as legal, accounting, or other professional services advice. While best efforts have been used in preparing this book, the author and publisher make no representations or warranties of any kind and assume no liabilities of any kind with respect to the accuracy or completeness of the contents and specifically disclaim any implied warranties of merchantability or fitness of use for a particular purpose. Neither the author nor the publisher shall be held liable or responsible to any person or entity with respect to any loss or incidental or consequential damages caused, or alleged to have been caused, directly or indirectly, by the information or programs contained herein. Nor shall the publisher or author be liable for any loss of profit or any other commercial damages, including but not limited to special, incidental, consequential, or other damages. No warranty may be created or extended by sales representatives or written sales materials. Every company is different and the advice and strategies contained herein may not be suitable for your situation. You should seek the services of a competent professional before beginning any improvement program. The author and publisher do not assume and hereby disclaim any liability to any party for any loss, damage, or disruption caused by errors or omissions, whether such errors or omissions result from negligence, accident, or any other cause.

DESCRIPTION

Have you ever dreamed of opening your own business but didn't know where to start? Are you tired of working hard for others? Have you ever had the desire to become an entrepreneur, but couldn't figure out just how to get started? Leave all your worries behind! *HELP! I'm Starting a New Business, A Step by Step Guide in Starting a New Business,* written by a successful entrepreneur has you covered! The information provided in this book is an easy, simple, and one-stop guide in assisting individuals who want to start a business, which gives you a step-by-step process in getting started. It covers all the fundamentals on stepping out on your dreams and starting your own business.

DEDICATION

I dedicate this book to every individual thinking, wishing, hoping, aspiring, and dreaming of opening a business and becoming a successful entrepreneur. May you exceed beyond what you have envisioned. Wishing you all the best in your business endeavors.

Contents

ACKNOWLEDGMENTS

Sincere thanks and gratitude to Debra Ricks-Sinquefield and Lynsie Battle for taking the time to skillfully edit this book for all readers to clearly grasp and understand the concepts and guidance provided.

INTRODUCTION

If you purchased this book, you are thinking about, considering, or are about to start a new business. Congratulations, you have taken the first step in starting a new business. Be proud of yourself! You are the individual that has dreamed of opening your own business but didn't know where to start; or maybe you are the individual that is tired of working hard for others and now wants to become your own boss; or the individual that desires to become an entrepreneur but couldn't figure out just how to do so, or the individual that is ready to start your business but needs guidance in doing so. Are you this person? You have all your ideas, concepts, and thoughts and are ready to go, but what now? *HELP! I'm Starting a New Business, A Step by Step Guide in Starting a New Business,* was written with you in mind and has you covered! This book is an easy, simple, direct, one-stop, step-by-step guide in assisting individuals like you who want to start a business. It covers all the fundamentals on stepping out on your dreams and starting your own business from start to finish. Now lets get to work!

Before filing for or creating a name or business, think about what entity you want your company to be which is a requirement. Common business entities are: Corporations (INC), General Partnerships (GP), Limited Liability Company's (LLC), Limited Partnerships (LP), Nonprofit Corporations, and Sole Proprietorships. The most common used entities are Corporations, LLC's, and Sole Proprietors. Be sure to fully understand which entity your business is before deciding.

You will also need to know if you have or will be utilizing a Trade Name or Doing Business As (DBA) name. You only have a trade name or DBA name IF your legal business name is NOT the name you are doing business as. For example, your legal business name may be "LOVE" but you may be doing business as "Lovely Dresses by Stephanie". Many organizations do not have a trade name or DBA; they just have a legal name, however some organizations do. It is completely up to you to decide.

HOW THIS BOOK IS ORGANIZED

HELP! I'm Starting a New Business, A Step by Step Guide in Starting a New Business, is organized so that you can easily access any information needed. The material is divided into seven parts. The seven parts effectively and directly explain the intricacies associated with starting a business in a detail oriented fashion. Throughout this book, I provide motivational quotes, tips, and sayings at the end of each chapter. This is simply to motivate you to continue to strive for the best while never giving up on your endeavors and aid in your business success. I also use fictitious business names, names, addresses, and telephone numbers to provide examples to better assist you when completing forms and to facilitate better understanding. When I use the term you, I am of course referring to you the reader, the business owner, or professional. When I use the term "mark" in *Chapter 6: Trade-Mark,* I am referring to the actual logo, design, or mark you are trying to trademark. Any verbiage that is bold or capitalized within each chapter is for you to pay special attention to. Enjoy!

CHAPTER 1

Business License

Obtaining a business license is typically the first step an entrepreneur takes in starting a business, as it is a requirement. A business license may also be known as an occupational tax license depending on your area of residence. When applying for your business license or occupational tax license, you will need to file it in the city where your business is located. You will need to contact the City Hall office in your local area and complete the application. The application is typically one page and consists of basic information. You will be charged a fee to apply for and renew a business license or occupational tax license. Your license is typically required to be renewed at the end of every year. When filing for your business license or occupational tax license, you may need to know what type of entity you or your business is or will be at the time of filing. If you have not decided which entity your business will be filed as, it is now time to decide. (A list of some entities are mentioned in the introduction part of this book).

"The future belongs to those who believe in the beauty of their dreams."

- Eleanor Roosevelt

CHAPTER 2

Employer Identification Number (EIN)

An Employer Identification Number (EIN) is required for all businesses within the United States of America, and all businesses need to obtain one. These numbers are issued for the purpose of tax administration. It is like a social security number for your business, it is a tax identifier and should be kept private. You may apply for your EIN number via phone, fax, mail, or online. The easiest and quickest way to obtain and apply for an EIN number is via the phone or the web. When filing for an EIN you need to know what type of entity you or your business is. If you are unsure what an entity is, please reference the introduction of this book which provides some entity examples. Once you have established what type of entity your business is you are ready to move forward.

Telephone (receive EIN immediately): You can receive your EIN by telephone and be able to use it immediately. Call the Internal Revenue Service toll free at 1-800-829-4933. Their hours of operation are 7:00 a.m. to 10:00 p.m. (Eastern Standard Time). The person making the call must be authorized to sign the form or be an authorized designee, which means they must be the owner, manager, or have some type of authority to receive the EIN and answer questions concerning the form SS-4, *Application for Employer Identification Number.* This form can be found http://www.irs.gov/uac/Form-SS-4,-Application-for-Employer-Identification-Number-(EIN). If you have no legal residence (or you are not a United States citizen), you may still apply for an EIN number via the phone but would need to call 267-941-1099 (this is not a toll free number) from 6:00 a.m. to 11:00 p.m. (Eastern Standard Time), Monday through Friday. This form can be found http://www.irs.gov/uac/Form-SS-4,-Application-for-Employer-Identification-Number-(EIN).

Fax (receive EIN within four (4) business days): You may fax a completed form called SS-4, *Application for Employer Identification Number.* This form can be found http://www.irs.gov/uac/Form-SS-4,-Application-for-Employer-Identification-Number-(EIN). When the form is completed in its entirety, fax it to Attention: EIN Operation Cincinnati, OH, 45999. The fax number is 859-669-5760 (this is not a toll free number). If your fax number is provided on your submittal, a fax will be sent back to you, which will contain your EIN within four (4) business days. If you have no legal residence (or you are not a United States citizen) you may still apply for an EIN number. Complete the form in its entirety and fax it to Attention: EIN Operation Philadelphia, PA 19255-0525. The fax number is 267-941-1040 (this is not a toll free number). If your fax number is provided, a fax will be sent back to you, which will contain your EIN within four (4) business days.

Mail (receive EIN within four (4) weeks): You may mail a completed form called SS-4, *Application for Employer Identification Number.* This form can be found http://www.irs.gov/uac/Form-SS-4,-Application-for-Employer-Identification-Number-(EIN). Complete the form in its entirety and mail it to:

Internal Revenue Service
Attn: EIN Operation
Cincinnati, OH 45999

If you have no legal residence (or you are not a United States citizen) you may still apply for your EIN number by mail. Complete the form in its entirety and mail it to:

Internal Revenue Service Attn:
EIN International Operation
Cincinnati, OH 45999

Be mindful that the processing timeframe for an EIN application received by mail is four weeks, so if you need your EIN earlier, this is not the option for you.

Online (receive EIN immediately): You can receive your EIN online and use it immediately. You may apply online at
https://sa1.www4.irs.gov/modiein/individual/index.jsp
If you are not comfortable sending information via the Internet, complete the form titles SS-4, *Application for Employer Identification Number* and submit via fax, mail, or telephone. This form can be located at
http://www.irs.gov/uac/Form-SS-4,-Application-for-Employer-Identification-Number-(EIN).

Steps to complete the Application SS-4:

There are a total of 18 steps.
RETAIN a copy of this application for your records.
Step 1: Type or write your legal business name; whatever it may be.
Step 2: If you have a trade name or DBA (doing business as name) you should enter it here. If your legal business is in fact your business name and you do not have a trade name or DBA name you would need to leave this area blank. For example, the name of my business may be *Hello Smiles* but my trade name or DBA name may be *Smiling Faces.* Many organizations do not have a trade name or DBA they just have a legal name; however some do.
Step 3: Type or write your name here. If someone other than yourself is completing the application on your behalf, they are considered to be

executors, administrators, or trustee's and their names should go here.

Step 4a: Type or write your business mailing address

Step 4b: Finish completing the business mailing address here

Step 5a: Type or write your street address here ONLY if it is different from Step 4a and Step 4b. If it is the same leave it blank.

Step 5b: Finish completing the street address here

Step 6: Type or write the county and state your business is located

Step 7a: Your name or the responsible parties name should go here.

Step 7b: Your Social Security number should go here or the responsible party that you placed in Step 7a their social security number should go here

Step 8a: If your business is an LLC, check "yes" here

Step 8b: If you selected "yes", then enter the members of your LLC., on this line If you are the only member enter one. If you are not the only member, enter the other member's names. If your business is not an LLC, then you do not need to compete this step.

Step 9a: Select the type of entity your business is. If your business is an LLC, you should have selected "yes" in step 8a on the form. (A list of some entities are mentioned in the introduction part of this book).

Step 9b: If you are a corporation complete this section by entering the state or foreign country where your business will be incorporated. If you are not a corporation, leave this section blank.

Step 10: Check the reason why you are applying for an EIN. The most common reason is *"started a new business"*.

Step 11: Here you should type or write the date the business started or the date you anticipate to start your business. Enter the date by month, day, and then year.

Step 12: You should type or write the closing month of your accounting year. Most people choose December because it is the end of the year and easier for accounting purposes; however you may select any month you prefer. You may also confer with your accountant, if you have one to see what closing month would be best for your business, but the month of December is most commonly used.

Step 13: Here you should type or write the number of employees you plan to have within 12 months. If it is none, put "0". If you plan to have employees within 12 months and it is not related to agricultural or household then place that number under "Other".

Step 14: If you expect your employment tax liability to be $1,000 or less in a full calendar year, you are eligible to file Form 944 annually (once each year) instead of filing Form 941 quarterly (every three months) which I recommend. Please remember if you file quarterly DO NOT FORGET to file. Most businesses that are just starting out, file yearly because they often forget and do not have much to pay if any. However, companies that make a substantial amount of money, file quarterly so that they will not have to pay a substantial amount of tax liability at one time. Your employment tax liability generally will be $1,000 or less if you expect to pay $4,000 or less in total wages. If you qualify and want to file Form 944 instead of Forms 941, check the box on line 14. If you do not check the box, then you must file Form 941 for every quarter. Generally, if you pay $6,536 or less in wages, you are likely to pay $1,000 or less in employment taxes so filing yearly would be recommended, so you may check the box if you want to file yearly.

Step 15: Here you should type or write the first date wages would be paid to employees. This is just an estimate and does not have to be exact. If you do not have employees or do not plan on having any employees, write that here. If you have or plan on having employees write the expected date here.

Step 16: Check the box that best describes your business activity meaning what your business does.

Step 17: Here you should write or type what you are selling, products or a service. Write exactly what you are selling or providing.

Step 18: Here you should write or type if you or your business has ever received an EIN number before. If you have, then select yes and write the EIN here; if you have not select no.

Now that you have completed the necessary steps, you must sign the application. Complete the "Third Party Designee", in its entirety ONLY if you want to authorize a person to receive your business EIN and answer questions about the completion of the SS-4 form on your behalf. If you are completing this application for you or your business type/write your name and title, telephone number, sign, and date the application. Write or type your fax number if you have one on the appropriate line (optional).

DO NOT FORGET to sign and date the form. It will not be processed unless it is signed and dated, which is under step 18.

Steps to complete Application SS-4 online:

(Use the above steps to aid in your online application)
There are 5 steps/sections when completing the application online.

1. Identity
2. Authenticate
3. Addresses
4. Details
5. EIN Confirmation

When those steps are complete, an EIN number will be provided. SAFEGUARD this number; as it is like your social security number for your business.

- Select "Begin Application".
- It should then direct you to a screen that states: "What type of legal structure are you applying for an EIN?" You may select the correct entity of your business. (A list of some entities are mentioned in the introduction part of this book).
- Then it may prompt you to a screen to confirm your selection.
- Once confirmed it will provide you with a description of your entity to be sure you are selecting the proper entity for your business.
- Then you select the reason for applying. Typically starting a new business is selected.
- Then it asks you to tell us about the Entity.
- Complete the form and questions asked.

When those steps are complete, an EIN number will be provided. SAFEGUARD this number; as it is like your social security number for your business and must be filed with your taxes, even if you have nothing to claim or report. Be mindful that in order to obtain a business bank account; you must have an EIN number.

In business, retain a copy of ALL INFORMATION, APPLICATIONS, FORMS, and DOCUMENTS pertaining to your business, even if you may think it is not significant. Please also note that when submitting documents, sometimes they may get lost and are never received, so it is very important to retain all records just in case you need to resubmit.

Copy of Actual SS-4 Form:

Form **SS-4**	**Application for Employer Identification Number**	OMB No. 1545-0003
(Rev. July 2007) Department of the Treasury Internal Revenue Service	(For use by employers, corporations, partnerships, trusts, estates, churches, government agencies, Indian tribal entities, certain individuals, and others.) ▶ See separate instructions for each line. ▶ Keep a copy for your records.	EIN

Type or print clearly.

1 Legal name of entity (or individual) for whom the EIN is being requested

2 Trade name of business (if different from name on line 1)	**3** Executor, administrator, trustee, "care of" name

4a Mailing address (room, apt., suite no. and street, or P.O. box)	**5a** Street address (if different) (Do not enter a P.O. box.)
4b City, state, and ZIP code (if foreign, see instructions)	**5b** City, state, and ZIP code (if foreign, see instructions)

6 County and state where principal business is located

7a Name of principal officer, general partner, grantor, owner, or trustor	**7b** SSN, ITIN, or EIN

8a Is this application for a limited liability company (LLC) (or a foreign equivalent)? ☐ Yes ☐ No **8b** If 8a is "Yes," enter the number of LLC members ▶

8c If 8a is "Yes," was the LLC organized in the United States? ☐ Yes ☐ No

9a Type of entity (check only one box). Caution. If 8a is "Yes," see the instructions for the correct box to check.

☐ Sole proprietor (SSN) _____
☐ Partnership
☐ Corporation (enter form number to be filed) ▶_____
☐ Personal service corporation
☐ Church or church-controlled organization
☐ Other nonprofit organization (specify) ▶_____
☐ Other (specify) ▶

☐ Estate (SSN of decedent) _____
☐ Plan administrator (TIN) _____
☐ Trust (TIN of grantor) _____
☐ National Guard ☐ State/local government
☐ Farmers' cooperative ☐ Federal government/military
☐ REMIC ☐ Indian tribal governments/enterprises
Group Exemption Number (GEN) if any ▶

9b If a corporation, name the state or foreign country (if applicable) where incorporated | State | Foreign country

10 Reason for applying (check only one box)
☐ Started new business (specify type) ▶ _____
☐ Hired employees (Check the box and see line 13.)
☐ Compliance with IRS withholding regulations
☐ Other (specify) ▶

☐ Banking purpose (specify purpose) ▶ _____
☐ Changed type of organization (specify new type) ▶ _____
☐ Purchased going business
☐ Created a trust (specify type) ▶ _____
☐ Created a pension plan (specify type) ▶ _____

11 Date business started or acquired (month, day, year). See instructions. **12** Closing month of accounting year

13 Highest number of employees expected in the next 12 months (enter -0- if none).

Agricultural	Household	Other

14 Do you expect your employment tax liability to be $1,000 or less in a full calendar year? ☐ Yes ☐ No (If you expect to pay $4,000 or less in total wages in a full calendar year, you can mark "Yes.")

15 First date wages or annuities were paid (month, day, year). Note. If applicant is a withholding agent, enter date income will first be paid to nonresident alien (month, day, year) ▶

16 Check **one** box that best describes the principal activity of your business. ☐ Health care & social assistance ☐ Wholesale-agent/broker
☐ Construction ☐ Rental & leasing ☐ Transportation & warehousing ☐ Accommodation & food service ☐ Wholesale-other ☐ Retail
☐ Real estate ☐ Manufacturing ☐ Finance & insurance ☐ Other (specify)

17 Indicate principal line of merchandise sold, specific construction work done, products produced, or services provided.

18 Has the applicant entity shown on line 1 ever applied for and received an EIN? ☐ Yes ☐ No
If "Yes," write previous EIN here ▶

Third Party Designee	Complete this section **only** if you want to authorize the named individual to receive the entity's EIN and answer questions about the completion of this form.	
	Designee's name	Designee's telephone number (include area code) ( )
	Address and ZIP code	Designee's fax number (include area code) ( )

Under penalties of perjury, I declare that I have examined this application, and to the best of my knowledge and belief, it is true, correct, and complete. | Applicant's telephone number (include area code)
( )

Name and title (type or print clearly) ▶ | Applicant's fax number (include area code)
( )

Signature ▶ Date ▶

For Privacy Act and Paperwork Reduction Act Notice, see separate instructions. Cat. No. 16055N Form **SS-4** (Rev. 7-2007)

CHAPTER 3

State Tax Registration

A state tax registration application is required in the United States of America. Each state has its own state tax registration form/application that you will need to complete in order to receive your number for your business. This form/application can be found at your state's Department of Revenues website or office under their registration and licensing unit. This form/application needs to be completed in order to have an operating business in the state your business is located. This form can be completed and submitted online, by fax, by email, or by mail depending on your state. This form allows you to register for a sales and use tax number, alcohol license, motor fuel license, withholding tax, if you are a lottery retailer, if you have a 911 prepaid wireless business, a limousine alcohol license, an amusement license, a non-resident distribution, a tobacco license, a motor carrier, a contractor, and to e-file/e-Pay Bulk Filer Registration. You may check more than one that may apply to your business now or your business in the future. Every business must be registered for a sales and use tax number to conduct business in the United States of America. When registering for a sales and use tax number and additional numbers or services you must have a:

1. Legal name, location, and mailing address of your business
2. Federal Identification Number (if applicable)
3. Tax account number (if it is an existing business)
4. Name and address of owners, partners, or officers
5. Social Security Number(s) of owners, partners, or officers
6. Email address (if available)

The State Tax Registration form typically has 8 sections

1.Reason For Submitting This Form (Identification Section)
2. Entity Type (a list of some entities are mentioned in the introduction part of this book)
3. Business Information
4. Business Mailing Address
5. Business Ownership/Relationship
6. Business Activity Information
7. Employer Withholding Information
8. Authorized Signature/Contact Information

Completing a State Tax Registration Application:

Section 1: Reason for Submitting this Form
Section one has eight questions. For questions one through five select one answer only. When completing this form for the first time and for a new

business you should select "New Registration", number one for the reason for this application. If you currently have a state tax registration and are looking for an additional registration number, master number, adding a location, or updating information you should check the box that applies and **not** select "New Registration". If you have four or more locations, you will need to select application for a Master Number (4 or more locations). In question six you should select "yes" or "no" to the questions that are asked. Most new businesses select "no" for all three questions under question six. Those questions ask if you acquired all or part of another business, select "yes" if you did, and select "no" if you did not. Question two asks if your business resulted from changing in legal structure (meaning are you changing the entity), if so select "yes", if not select "no". Question three asks if your business is undergoing a merger, consolidation, dissolution, or other restricting, if so, select "yes", if not select "no". Question seven only needs to be answered if you answered, "yes" to any questions in number six. Question number eight is next. Here you select all that applies to your business (you may select more than one). For all new businesses and new business owners, a sales and use tax number is required and must be selected in order to have an operating business in the United States of America. A withholding tax number is required if you plan on hiring employees now or in the future. You can always go back and apply for a withholding tax at a later date, but if you have employees or know you are going to have employees in the future, select withholding tax in addition to sales and use. You may also select the other taxes or services only if they fit your business. Again, sales and use tax must be selected, but if other taxes pertain to your business, you may select them now, at your own discretion.

Section 2: Entity Type
In this section you should select your business entity.

Section 3: Business Information
This is where your business information should go. In part one, enter your legal business name or your name if you are a sole proprietor. If you have a trade name or DBA (doing business as name), you should enter it on the line where asked. If your legal business is in fact your business name and you do not have a trade name or DBA name, you would need to leave that area blank. Continue completing this section, which asks for your business street address (which may be your home), city, county, state, zip code, telephone number (which may be your cellular phone), fax number (if you have one), and your email. It will also ask for your first date of operation, or the date you plan to operate, or open your business. If your business is a seasonal business, list the months of the season where asked. Questions four and five refer to the accounting aspects of your business. It asks about

your fiscal year end and your accounting method. It also asks you which method of accounting should you use, cash basis or accrual basis (which is further explained in this section). Select which method pertains to your business preferences. You must also indicate the last month and day of your accounting year. Most people pick December 31, because it is the end of the year and easier for accounting purposes. However, select whatever date you prefer. If you have one, you may also talk to your accountant to see what month would be best to close out your business, but December is the most commonly used month. If you are unsure which accounting method to utilize; accrual or cash, you may confer with your accountant, if you have one for further assistance. If you do not have an accountant to help you better understand the difference between the cash or accrual method, the cash method is the most commonly used by small businesses. Income is not counted until payment/money is received and expenses are not counted until they are actually paid. Under the accrual method transactions are accounted for when the order is made, delivered, and services occur, regardless of when payment is received. Income is counted when sales occur and expenses are counted when goods or services are received. You do not have to actually have the money to record the transaction.

For example, lets say your business phone installation is completed in April but you don't pay until July. With the cash method, you should record the payment in July, when they are actually paid. With the accrual method you should record the payment in April once its actually installed. You must however, use the accrual method if your business has over five million dollars in sales per year or if your business stocks inventory items that you will sell to the public in which your gross receipts are over one million per year. Most new businesses select the "cash" accounting method however, you must decide which is best for your business.

Section 4: Business Mailing Address
This is **only** to be completed if your business mailing address is different from what was entered in section three or if you want other correspondence for a specific tax type that you selected in section 1 mailed to an address other than the address provided in section three. You should write/enter the address and select the specified tax types.

Section 5: Business Ownership/Relationship (typically shown twice)
This section focuses on the business ownership/relationship. Information in this section that does not apply to you should be left blank. In this section two owners can be included. When completing this section you should enter the business owners information. If there is more than one owner another owner can be entered in the duplicated area. If there is just one owner then the duplicated area should remain blank.

Section 6: Business Activity Information

This is the business activity information section. This section addresses the nature of your business and requires basic information regarding your business activity. The first part will ask you to check the business activity type(s), which are retail, manufacturing, wholesale, construction, and service. If you select one activity then you should write 100% next to that activity, as this is solely what your business is, operates, and does 100 % of the time. If you select more than one box then you must divide the percentages up, they must equate to 100% . For example if you are in retail you should select retail and write in 100%. If your business is half retail and half wholesale you should need to select both and write 50% for retail and 50% for wholesale or 70% retail and 30% wholesale depending the percentage that accurately reflects the scope of your business. Question two asks if you will be selling motor fuel or gasoline, you should answer that question, if it applies. Question three asks if you are a common carrier; answer this question if it applies. Question 4 asks for you to describe the products or services you will be providing, list those services here. Question five asks for your North American Industry Classification System (NAICS) code number if you know it (you may leave this blank if you do not know it) all NAICS codes can be found at: http://www.naics.com/

Section 7: Employer Withholding Information

This section should be completed if you are applying for a withholding number, and are going to have employees. You should select "yes" to question one. If you are not going to have employees or are not applying for a withholding number, select "no" and do not answer any further questions in this section. If you selected "yes" complete the rest of the questions in this section by stating who is responsible for your businesses payroll. If it is a payroll service you would need to provide their name, withholding tax account number, if you have it; if it is not a payroll company, leave this question blank. The next question asks if you expect to withhold more than $200.00 per month with your payroll service; select "yes" or "no", whichever applies. The last question in this section asks you to select the first date that wages will be paid to employees. If you know the exact date, enter it here. If not, enter the expected date (month, year, or both) or if you are unsure you may enter "unsure".

Section 8: Authorized Signature/Contact Information

In this section you must sign your name, print your name, date, title, and telephone number. If you have a third party preparer, you may list that person here as well and be sure to include their title and telephone number.

Some states have an additional form(s) attached to the application/form, which is the "Responsible Party Information". This information must be completed as it identifies the specific responsible party or the person that is responsible for the business. Complete that form in its entirety. Please be sure to make copies of this form once completed prior to submission. Safeguard your tax numbers and do not share them with anyone, as these are important to your business. Please also remember that taxes must be filed quarterly or yearly depending on how it is set up for your business.

"Being an entrepreneur is living a few years of your life like most people wont so that you can spend the rest of your life living like most people cant."

- Unknown

An example of a "State Tax Registration Application" is located here:

Form CRF-002 (Rev. 2/12)

GEORGIA DEPARTMENT OF REVENUE
REGISTRATION & LICENSING UNIT
P. O. BOX 49512
ATLANTA, GEORGIA 30359-1512
Fax: 404-417-4317 OR 404-417-4318
NEED HELP? CALL 1 (877) 423-6711
E-MAIL: ST-License@dor.ga.gov
TSD-withholding-ioi@dor.ga.gov

1203904011

Page 1

Georgia Department of Revenue

State Tax Registration Application

Section 1   Reason for Submitting this Form

Refer to the instructions and check the applicable box(es) to indicate the reason(s) for this registration.

1. ☐ New Registration
2. ☐ Additional Registration
3. ☐ Application for a Master Number
4. ☐ Information Update
5. ☐ Additional Location
   (Use only for Master Sales Tax Account)

6. Did your business:

☐ Yes ☐ No Acquire all or part of another business?

☐ Yes ☐ No Result from a change in legal structure (for example, from individual proprietor to corporation, partnership to corporation, corporation to limited liability company, etc...)?

☐ Yes ☐ No Undergo a merger, consolidation, dissolution, or other restructuring?

7. Provide prior business' state tax identification number if you answered yes to any of the above choices:

8. Check the applicable box(es) to indicate the types of tax(es) and service(s) requested for this registration. Those types with asterisks (**) require an additional application.

☐ Sales and Use
☐ Withholding Tax
☐ Alcohol License**
☐ Tobacco License**
☐ Lottery Retailer**
☐ 911 Prepaid Wireless
☐ Limousine Alcohol License **
☐ Non-Resident Distribution
☐ Amusement License **
☐ Motor Fuel License**
☐ Motor Carrier/IFTA
☐ Contractor

Section 2   Entity Type *(check the appropriate box)*

☐ Sole Proprietorship (Individual)
☐ Professional Association
☐ Limited Liability Partnership
☐ Partnership
☐ Estate
☐ Federal Agency
☐ Sub-S Corporation
☐ Fiduciary
☐ State Agency
☐ Corporation- State of Incorporation: ____ Incorporation Date:_____
☐ Limited Liability Company ☐ Single Member ☐ Multiple Member
☐ County Government
☐ Municipal Government

Section 3   Business Information

1. Business Legal Name *(enter owner's name if sole proprietor)*	Business Trade Name (DBA)		Federal Employer Information Number	
Business Street Address **(DO NOT USE P.O. BOX)**	City	County	State	Zip Code + 4
Business Telephone Number	Business Fax Number	Business Email		

2. Date of First Operation (mm/dd/yyyy): _____
3. List months of operation if business is seasonal (mm-mm): _____
4. List Business's Fiscal Year End: _____
5. Identify Accounting Method: ☐ Accrual   ☐ Cash

Section 4   Business Mailing Address *(if different from Section 3 above)*

If you want to have GADOR notices and other correspondence for a specific tax type mailed to an address other than the above business street address, please complete the following information. Use Form CRF-003 to list additional addresses.

1. Business Mailing Address	City	County	State	Zip Code + 4

2. Use this mailing address for the following tax type(s):
☐ Sales and Use ☐ Withholding ☐ Amusement ☐ Alcohol ☐ Tobacco ☐ Motor Fuel Distributor ☐ 911 Prepaid Wireless

1. Business Mailing Address	City	County	State	Zip Code + 4

2. Use this mailing address for the following tax type(s):
☐ Sales and Use ☐ Withholding ☐ Amusement ☐ Alcohol ☐ Tobacco ☐ Motor Fuel Distributor ☐ 911 Prepaid Wireless

Section 5   Business Ownership/Relationship

1. Name	Social Security Number / Taxpayer Identification Number		
Mailing Address	City	County	State	Zip Code + 4

Check one:
☐ Owner ☐ LLC Member ☐ Partner ☐ Officer ☐ Other   Effective Date: _____

Check any/all if applicable:
☐ Alcohol Licensee   Effective Date: _____   ☐ Tobacco Licensee   Effective Date : _____

CHAPTER 4

Employer Status Report

This chapter will only be beneficial to you if your business has employees or you plan to have employees at a later date. If you do not have employees or plan to have employees, you may proceed to Chapter 5. If you do have employees, an employer status report must be completed with the Department of Labor in the state your business is located. To complete this report you will need to know all your basic business information including your Federal Identification Number, date employees started or plan to start, date of your first payroll, and if you are liable for federal unemployment tax (for most small businesses the answer should be "no"). The report must be completed and returned to your states Department of Labor via mail. Some states allow you to complete the report via the web and/or fax.

Completing an Employer Status Report:

Part 1:

The first question asks you to enter your business name and address. The second question asks for your Department of Labor Account Number and the type or organization/entity your business is (a list of some entities are mentioned in the introduction part of this book). If you do not have your Department of Labor Account Number, you may leave it blank, as it is not required. Question three asks for your business trade name, if you do not have a trade name or DBA, leave this area blank. Question four asks for your business physical address and telephone number. Question five asks when your employee's will begin work and date of first payroll; an estimated time is fine if you are not exactly certain. Question six asks if you are liable for federal unemployment tax which most new business select "no" and it also asks for your federal Identification Number, which is your EIN number. Question seven asks the following questions in which most businesses respond "no". Have you acquired another business, merged with another business, formed a corporation or partnership, or made any other change in the business ownership. These are "yes" or "no" questions. If you answered "no" for all three questions move on to question eight. If you answered "yes" for any of the above questions, then more questions would follow depending on what question was answered "yes". Those questions are: what is the date you acquired the business; if you merged a business what was the predecessor's previous Department of Labor number, and does the former owner continue to have employees. The next part asks did you acquire all of the operations, substantially all of your state operations (90% or more), or part of the operations (less than 90%). If the business was acquired from another company you would have to state the business and the address. Question 8 asks the following questions in which most business reply "no" however, if the statement applies to your business, be sure to select "yes". Did you or do you expect to employ one worker in 20 different calendar weeks during a calendar year? (If you select yes, a date must be provided). Did you or do you expect to have a quarterly payroll of $1,500.00 or more? If yes, provide the date this first occurred. Question nine asks if you had domestic employment and did you, or do you expect to pay cash wages of $1,000.00 or more in any calendar quarter? If yes, then provide the date first occurred. Question ten asks if you had agricultural employment? Meaning did you, or do you expect to employ 10 or more agricultural workers in 20 different calendar weeks during a calendar year. If yes, show date the 20th week first occurred. It also asks, did you or do you expect to have a gross cash agricultural payroll of $20,000 or more in any calendar quarter? If yes, provide documentation on the date this first occurred. Question eleven asks if you are a nonprofit exempt from tax code 501(C)(3): Did you, or do you expect to employ four or more workers in 20 different calendar weeks during a calendar year? If you select yes, you must attach your 501 (C)(3) letter and provide the date the 20th week first occurred. Question twelve is a three-part inquiry. It asks how many employees do you have or intend to have when in full operation? You are then asked to provide information pertaining to the owner, all partners, or principal offer(s). Then you are asked to provide information on the person or firm who maintains financial records of the business. If you will be using a payroll service, include that information there. If you are not using a payroll company your information should be entered here or the person who maintains that particular information should go here. You must also sign, date, and write your title where indicated.

Part 2:
Consists of the "Nature of your business". This section typically has four parts to complete (A-D). Part A asks how many locations you operate? If your business has more than one location place that information here. Part B asks you to check the box that best describes the industry that relates to your business activities. Once this is complete the other 2 sections (C and D) typically do not apply to new businesses and can remain blank, however, if they apply to you, then they must be completed. Those questions are: enter in order of importance and indicate the approximate % of total income derived from each principal service renders or principal product. Then if this report includes establishments that only perform services for other units of the company, indicate the primary type of service or support provided. Check as many as possible that applies to your business (options should be provided). Once this form is complete make a copy and submit it. The report must be completed and returned to your states Department of Labor via mail. Some states allow you to complete the form via the web and/or fax it in once completed, but other states require that the form be mailed in.

An example of an "Employer Status Report" is located below:

GEORGIA DEPARTMENT OF LABOR
SUITE 850 - 148 ANDREW YOUNG INTERNATIONAL BLVD NE - ATLANTA, GA 30303-1751

EMPLOYER STATUS REPORT

READ INSTRUCTIONS ON REVERSE SIDE
BEFORE COMPLETION OF FORM

1. ENTER OR CORRECT BUSINESS NAME AND ADDRESS

RETURN ORIGINAL WITHIN 10 DAYS

GEORGIA DOL
ACCOUNT NUMBER ☐☐☐☐☐☐ – ☐☐
(If already assigned)

3. TRADE NAME

2. TYPE OF ORGANIZATION

☐ Individual ☐ Partnership ☐ Corporation ☐ Nonprofit org.
☐ Limited Liability CO. (LLC)
☐ Other (specify)

4. PRINCIPAL BUSINESS, FARM OR HOUSEHOLD LOCATION IN GEORGIA (Do not use a P. O. Box number)

Street Address				
City		Zip Code	County	Telephone Number
	GA			( )

5. DATE FIRST BEGAN EMPLOYING WORKERS WITHIN STATE OF GA. — DATE OF FIRST GA. PAYROLL

6. ARE YOU LIABLE FOR FEDERAL UNEMPLOYMENT TAX? Yes ☐ No ☐

FEDERAL I.D. NUMBER ☐☐ – ☐☐☐☐☐☐☐

7. HAVE YOU...

Acquired another business? Yes ☐ No ☐

DATE ACQUIRED OR CHANGED

Merged with another business? Yes ☐ No ☐

PREDECESSOR'S GEORGIA DOL ACCOUNT NUMBER ☐☐☐☐☐☐ – ☐☐

Formed a corporation or partnership? Yes ☐ No ☐

DOES THE FORMER OWNER CONTINUE TO HAVE EMPLOYEES? Yes ☐ No ☐

Made any other change in the ownership of your business? Yes ☐ No ☐ If yes, explain _____

DID YOU ACQUIRE...
☐ All of Georgia operations?
☐ Substantially all of Georgia operations (90% or more)
☐ Part of Georgia operations (less than 90%)

FROM WHOM? (Organization name, including trade name)

ADDRESS

8. IF YOU HAD PRIVATE BUSINESS EMPLOYMENT:
Did you, or do you expect to employ at least one worker in 20 different calendar weeks during a calendar year? Yes * ☐ No ☐
* If yes, show date the 20th week first occurred:

Did you, or do you expect to have a quarterly payroll of $1,500 or more? Yes * ☐ No ☐
* If yes, show date this first occurred:

11. IF YOU ARE A NONPROFIT ORGANIZATION EXEMPT FROM INCOME TAX UNDER IRS CODE 501(C)(3): Yes * ☐ No ☐
Did you, or do you expect to employ four or more workers in 20 different calendar weeks during a calendar year? (ATTACH COPY OF 501(C)(3) EXEMPTION LETTER)
* If yes, show date the 20th week first occurred:

9. IF YOU HAD DOMESTIC EMPLOYMENT:
Did you, or do you expect to pay cash wages of $1,000 or more in any calendar quarter? Yes* ☐ No ☐
* If yes, show date this first occurred:

10. IF YOU HAD AGRICULTURAL EMPLOYMENT: Yes* ☐ No ☐
Did you, or do you expect to employ 10 or more agricultural workers in 20 different calendar weeks during a calendar year?
* If yes, show date the 20th week first occurred:

Did you, or do you expect to have a gross cash agricultural payroll of $20,000 or more in any calendar quarter? Yes* ☐ No ☐
* If yes, show date this first occurred:

12. HOW MANY EMPLOYEES do you have, (or anticipate when in full operation)?

INFORMATION ABOUT OWNER, ALL PARTNERS, OR PRINCIPAL OFFICER (ATTACH ADDITIONAL SHEET, OR SHEETS, IF NECESSARY)

Name		
Social Security Number ☐☐☐ – ☐☐ – ☐☐☐☐		
Residence Address		
City		
State	Zip Code	
Telephone ( )		

INFORMATION ABOUT PERSON OR FIRM WHO MAINTAINS FINANCIAL RECORDS OF BUSINESS

Name		
Address		
City		
State	Zip Code	Telephone ( )

CERTIFICATION: I hereby certify under penalties of perjury, that the foregoing statement and those contained in any attached sheets signed by me are true and correct, and that I am authorized to execute this report on behalf of the employing unit. This report must be signed by owner, partner or principal officer.

Signature	Title	Date

PLEASE COMPLETE INDUSTRY INFORMATION ON REVERSE SIDE.

DOL-1A (R-5/05)
TA489A

"Hardships often prepare ordinary people for an extraordinary destiny."

- C.S. Lewis

CHAPTER 5

Secretary of State

When opening or starting a business, some states require that you register with the Secretary of State in the state your business is located. However, if you are a sole proprietor, registering with the Secretary of State may not be a requirement. If your business is a limited liability company, a corporation, or a partnership, then in most states, it is a requirement for you to register your business with the state. If you are not ready to actually register your business with the Secretary of State, you may file the name and reserve the name for a fee. A name may be reserved prior to filing, but a name reservation is not required to file.

Registering

To register with the Secretary of State, go to your states Secretary of States website. Each state has there own website and all filings can be filed online. It is fairly simple to register online and the information needed is basic pertaining to your business. Before filing, you will need to know your business entity status (a list of some entities are mentioned in the introduction part of this book). To start, you will need to go to online services and select "file online". On this page you may conduct a search to be sure the name of your business is not already in use by another party. In order to proceed with registering, some state websites require an account to be created, if so create a log in (free cGov360) account, and, of course, retain this information for future use. Once an account is created, go to business filing and select the type of filing you would like to file. Once selected you should read the filing procedures. Once you have read the filing procedures select "Next". If you ordered a name reservation (which means you had your business name on hold so no one else could use it), enter your name reservation number and select "Next". If not, simply select "Next" to continue. At this point you should be on the "Filer" page. Complete this page in its entirety. You will then continue to the "Index" page, complete this form in its entirety. Proceed by selecting "Next", once the form is complete. You are now at the "Organizer" page. Complete this page in its entirety. Keep in mind a lot of information may be repetitive if you are the only person in your business, such as business address, registered Agent (which should be you), or event contact type (which may be you as well). You should now be at the "Signature Block" page. Complete this page and add a signer if needed (someone else, other than you, who may sign off and plays an important role in your business). Then select "Next". This will prompt the "Expedite" page. While this is optional, it can be useful for business owners who prefer not to wait the standard timeframe. "Validation" should be the page you are now on. Verify that all information is accurate. Proceed by selecting "Next" on to the payment page. Provide payment details and information then proceed to the next step. Save and print all information provided to include forms. Be mindful that this registration must be renewed yearly. Also be mindful that in order to obtain a business bank account you must be registered with the Secretary of State. After registering, some states require additional information once registration is complete. If you are a sole proprietor, there are typically no additional requirements needed in most states if registration was required. Additional Articles are needed for a Limited Liability Company (LLC), Corporation (INC), Nonprofit, Limited Partnership (LP), and State Franchise. If you are filing an Incorporation then Articles of Incorporation need to accompany and remain in the file. Furthermore, depending on the state your business is located in the Articles of Incorporation must also be published in the local paper. If filing a LLC, Articles of Organization will need to always remain in your file and may be requested by the Secretary of State.

Renewal

When renewing with the Secretary of State, you must log into your account that you received upon registering. From the home page, select "edit", and add the report year (or current year) when prompted. Lastly, verify all information, and submit payment. If you need to change any information this is the time to do so. Renewal fees are typically $50.00 but may vary.

Articles

Some states require additional information once registration is complete. If you have a sole proprietor there are no additional articles needed in most states. However, additional articles are needed for a Limited Liability Company (LLC), Corporation (INC), Nonprofit, Limited Partnership (LP), and State Franchise in most states. An example of some of those can be found in this chapter. Typically the articles need to be mailed to the Secretary of State, but may not be required by all states. Always keep a copy for your records.

Publication of Notice of Intent to Incorporate

Corporations must publish a notice of intent to incorporate in the newspaper which can be known as the official legal organ of the county where the initial registered office of the business/corporation is located or will be located. It can also be published in a newspaper of general circulation in the county for which at least 60 percent of its subscriptions are paid (an example of a notice of incorporation is located in this chapter). If your state requires you to do so, a list of legal organs or papers will be provided on the Secretary of States website, or the Clerk of Superior Court can advise you which paper or legal organ to publish in your county. The Notice of Intent to Incorporate and a publication fee should be forwarded directly to the newspaper no later than the next business day after filing.

Example of Articles of Organization for a LLC

Articles of Organization of Smiles and Associates, LLC

Article 1.

The name of the Limited Liability Company is Smiles and Associates, LLC.

(Note: Article 2. below is optional. It, and other provisions not inconsistent with law, may be set forth in the Articles of Organization.)

Article 2.

Management of the limited liability company is vested in one or more managers whose names and addresses are as follows:

Enter Names Here

IN WITNESS WHEREOF, the undersigned has executed these Articles of Organization.

This _____ day of _____, 2015

(Signature)

Name printed of signature here

(Capacity/Title of signer)

Example of Articles of Incorporation for a Profit Corporation

Articles of Incorporation of Smiles and Associates, Inc.

Article 1

The name of the corporation is Smiles and Associates, Inc.

Article 2

The corporation is authorized to issue (fill in the number) shares. *(Number may not be "0".)*

Article 3

The street address of the registered office is 123 Smiles Lane, Griffin, Georgia 56789. The registered agent at such address is Chris Doe. *(The registered office address must be a physical address at which the agent may be personally located.)* The county of the registered office is _____.

Article 4

The name and address of each incorporator is:

Chris Doe
123 Smiles Lane
Griffin, Georgia 56789

Chrissie Doe
123 Smiles Lane
Griffin, Georgia 56789

Christopher Doe
123 Smiles Lane
Griffin, Georgia 56789

Article 5

The principal mailing address of the corporation is 123 Smiles Lane, Griffin, Georgia 56789 (this may be a P.O. Box).

IN WITNESS WHEREOF, the undersigned has executed these Articles of Incorporation on the _____day of _____, 2015.

(Signature)

Chris Doe (Capacity of signer
i.e. incorporator
or attorney)

Example of Articles of Incorporation for Nonprofit Corporation

Articles of Incorporation of

Smiles and Associates, Inc.

Article 1

The name of the corporation is Smiles and Associates, Inc.

Article 2

The corporation is organized pursuant to the Georgia Nonprofit Corporation Code.

Article 3

The street address of the registered office is 123 Smiles Lane, Griffin, Georgia 56789. The registered agent at such address is Chris Doe. *(The registered office address must be a physical address at which the agent may be personally located.)* The county of the registered office is _____.

Article 4

The name and address of each incorporator is:

Chris Doe	Chrissie Doe	Christopher Doe
123 Smiles Lane	123 Smiles Lane	123 Smiles Lane
Griffin, Georgia 56789	Griffin, Georgia 56789	Griffin, Georgia 56789
		56789

Article 5

The corporation (will/will not) have members.

Article 6

The principal mailing address of the corporation is 123 Smiles Lane, Griffin, Georgia 12345.

IN WITNESS WHEREOF, the undersigned has executed these Articles of Incorporation on the _____day of _____, 2015.

(Signature)

Chris Doe (Capacity of signer
(i.e. incorporator or attorney in fact))

Example of Articles of Certificate of Limited Partnership

Must be signed by all partners.

Certificate of Limited Partnership

of

Smiles and Associates, L.P.

1.

The name of the limited partnership is Smiles and Associates, L.P..

2.

The street address of the registered office is 12345 Smiles Lane, Griffin, Georgia 56789, in Coweta County. The registered agent at such address is Chris Doe.

(The registered office address must be a street address.)

3.

The name and address of each general partner is:

Chris Doe 123 Smiles Lane Griffin, Georgia 56789	Chrissie Doe 123 Smiles Lane Griffin, Georgia

IN WITNESS WHEREOF, the undersigned has executed this Certificate of Limited Partnership.

This _____ day of _____, 2015.

(Signature)

Chris Doe

(Capacity in which person is signing)

Notice of Incorporation (for the county newspapers or legal organs)

Dear Publisher:

Please publish once a week, for two consecutive weeks, a notice in the following form:

Notice is given that Articles of Incorporation that will incorporate Smiles and Associates, Inc. have been delivered to the Secretary of State for filing in accordance with the (insert your state here) Business Corporation Code or (insert your state here) Nonprofit Corporation Code (if applicable). The initial registered office of the corporation is located at 123 Smiles Lane, Griffin, Georgia 56789, and its initial registered agent at such address is Chris Doe.

Enclosed is (check, draft or money order) in the amount of $(Insert amount here) in payment of the cost of publishing this notice.

Sincerely,

(Authorized signature)

Chris Doe

"Let your success be your noise, work hard in silence."

- Unknown

CHAPTER 6

Trademark

Trademarks are not a requirement to start or have in a business. Most businesses trademark their logo and/or name so that it cannot be used by anyone else. To file you must have access to a computer with high speed Internet and $325.00. Trademarks may be filed online at The United States Patent and Trademark Office (USPTO) (http://www.uspto.gov/trademarks/). Before starting you should conduct an electronic search to be sure the mark you want to file is not already in use by using the link above. Once you have used the above link select TESS (Trademark Electronic Search System) to search for the mark. When you have confirmed that the mark is available, you may continue with filing via the USPTO website. There are eight parts to complete when filing a trademark online, which are: Applicant Information, Mark Information, Basis for Filing, Correspondence Information, Fee Information, Electronic Signature, Declaration, and a Validation Page. When filing a trademark you are given 60 minutes to complete the application. However, an application may be saved during the completion at any time if needed.

Steps for applying for Trademark/Service Mark Application, Principal Register

In order to file for a trademark you must have an updated Internet browser that has the cookies and JavaScript features of your browser enabled. When completing the form, do **not** use your browser's **"BACK"** or **"FORWARD"** buttons at any time to navigate through any portion of the application. Always use the navigational tools provided at the bottom of the form pages. Only **one** mark per application is allowed to be submitted. Before the USPTO can register the mark, you need to know what type of mark you will be filing. There are three types of marks: standard character, special form, or a sound mark. Below are descriptions of each:

1. **Standard Character**- is used if you are not claiming a particular design element, font, style, size, and/or color. This basically means you would be trademarking the name not the style or the design. It is a mark that contains words only and no matter how it is written be it font size, font style, or the colors used in the mark, you would be trademarking the name because you do not want it used by anyone else. A JPG image of the mark is required.

2. **Special Form**- is a mark that should be used if your mark includes a design or has word(s) combined with a design, or if your mark is displayed in a particular font, style, size, and/or color. For example, if your companies name is "Smiles" and your logo/mark is the word "Smiles" with an image of a "smiley face" you should use this type of mark. A JPG image of the mark is required.

3. **Sound Mark** - a sound mark is a non-visual mark, which is either a sound or motion mark. If you have a sound mark, the mark must be in the following electronic files .wav, .wmv, .wma, .mp3, .mpg, or .avi. The file should only contain the sound and must not exceed 5MB for an audio file and 30MG for a video file. An understandable description of the mark must also be entered in the appropriate field explaining details of the mark.

Once you understand and know the type of mark you want to file you may start the trademark filing process by going to http://www.uspto.gov/trademarks/ and selecting "TEAS (Trademark Electronic Application SYSTEM (TEAS)". Once the TEAS page populates, select "Initial Application Form". Then select "Trademark/Service Mark Application, Principal Register". You now should be at the "Selection of Application Type" page. Select the TEAS Form which is $325.00 and select continue, do not select the TEAS Plus Form, unless you are familiar and are certain that your mark qualifies for the TEAS Plus Form requirements. You now should be at the Trademark/Service Mark Application, Principal Register. Read the instructional information provided by The United States Patent and Trademark Office to aid in understanding.

Application: (The application starts with two questions)
1. Answer yes or no to the question regarding if an attorney will be filing this application. If you are filing then the answer should be "no" unless you are an attorney.
2. The next question pertains to you previously saving an application that has not yet been completed. If you have previously saved your application, you may complete it at this time.

Applicant Information
Complete the applicant's information. This information is regarding the individual filing and your business. If there is more than one owner, this may be added at the end of the page.

Mark Information
If your mark is a Standard Character mark then that mark should be selected, proceed and enter the mark in the appropriate box. Select continue if you do not have an additional statement to add. If you have an additional statement to add about your mark enter it, and then select continue to proceed with the application.

If your mark is a Special Form (stylized and/or design) then select this type of mark. Choose the file where your mark is located, and then select attach. If your mark image includes verbiage enter it in the appropriate area on the form. If claiming color as a feature of the mark, list all colors (meaning your mark will contain specific colors when used). If you are not claiming color (meaning you want to use the mark regardless of the color or it does not contain color) select the box that states you will NOT be claiming color. Describe your mark in the last box on this form. Select continue if you do not have an additional statement to add. If you have an additional statement to add about your mark enter it, and then select continue to proceed with the application.

If your mark is a Sound mark select this type of mark. Choose the file where your mark is located and then select attach. Describe your mark in the last box on this form. Select continue if you do not have any additional information to add. If you have an additional statement to add enter it, and then select continue to proceed with the application.

Basis for Filing
You should now be at the Goods and/or Services Information. Select option one, "Searching ID Manual". Then select "Add Goods/Services". This is where you select what the trademark is used for be it, shoes, food, clothing, etc. Type in the search (what your mark is for). When the entries come up check all that apply to your mark. Be very detailed. Then select "Insert checked entries".

The next step identifies the choices of filing basis to be assigned. Select Section 1(a), (b), 44 (d), or (e). Explanations are located under each. If you select Section 1(a) you are stating the mark is already in use. 1(b) you intend to use it, 44(d) you have a foreign application and it exists for the same goods/services, and 44(e) you have an actual registration that exists for the same goods/services.

If selecting Section 1(a):
You must attach an actual image showing the mark is in use and explain what it is used on (website, box, etc). You must then provide the dates the mark has been in use, the official start date.

If selecting Section 1(b):
Proceed with selecting the statement of understanding.
You may not select both

If selecting Section 1(a) or Section 1(b), only one may be selected it must be one or the other. However, you may select Section 1(a) **OR** If selecting Section 1(b) **AND** Section 44 (d) or (e).
Select continue.

Correspondence Information

You should now be at the Correspondence Information Page. There are two questions at the top, check if they apply. Because you are completing this yourself neither question should apply. Review the correspondence information and be sure all information is accurate. Docket/Reference Number and Firm name more than likely will **NOT** apply to you. (**Docket/Reference Number:** If applicable, enter the docket or reference number. **Firm Name:** The name of the company or firm for the address of the correspondent.)

Fee Information, Electronic Signature, DECLARATION

You should now be at the Fee Information Page. You may proceed with the "sign directly signature" if you choose to, or select the signature choice you prefer. Continue to declaration and proceed with signing.

Under Signature type the forward slash symbol "/" and your name and then add another forward slash symbol "/". DO NOT HIT THE SPACE BAR AFTER THE forward slash symbol "/".

Under Signatory's Name type your name

Under Signatory's Position Type your title ("President," "General Partner," etc.) or the relationship to the applicant ("Manager," "Trademark Administrator", etc.). If an individual applicant signing on his or her own behalf, enter "Owner." If an attorney, enter "Attorney of record, [specify at least one state] bar member;" to help confirm that you are authorized to sign, you must enter the name of at least one state in which you have active bar membership. Please note that "state" includes the District of Columbia, Puerto Rico, and other federal territories and possessions. Please know that you do not have to be an attorney to file a trademark.

Under "Signatory's Phone Number" type your phone number or business number

Date the form and select "Validate" unless you need to add additional signatures.

Validation Page

You should now be at the validation page. Review the application data in various formats, by selecting on the phrases under Application Data. Use the print function within your browser to print these pages for your own records.

On this page you may continue to pay and submit, download portable data, or go back to modify. You must also verify that your email address is correct. I recommend that you download your portable data for your records. Be sure to read the important notice and select the box once read. Select the Pay/Submit button **if you** are prepared to complete the process. After selecting the button, you **cannot** return to the form. You now should be out of the TEAS site entirely. Once on the separate payment site, you **must** complete the Pay/Submit process within **30 minutes.** If you are not prepared to complete the process now, you should select the "Download Portable Data" option to save your form, and then complete the "Pay/Submit" process at a later date or time. If you have discovered any errors, use the "Go Back to Modify" button to make a correction.

Please keep in mind that once you receive your certificate of registration (principal register) to avoid cancelation in the future, you would need to submit a declaration of continued use or excusable non-use between the fifth and sixth year after the registration date. Basically by submitting a declaration of continued use, you will be renewing your trademark when it expires.

"The pessimist sees difficulty in every opportunity. The optimist sees the opportunity in every difficulty."

- Unknown

An example of a "Standard Character Mark":

United States of America
United States Patent and Trademark Office

FEVƎR

Reg. No. 4,181,694

Registered July 31, 2012

Int. Cl.: 25

TRADEMARK

PRINCIPAL REGISTER

FOR: FOOTWEAR, EXCLUDING FOOTWEAR FOR COSTUMES AND DRESS-UP, IN CLASS 25 (U.S. CLS. 22 AND 39).

FIRST USE 3-1-2010; IN COMMERCE 4-1-2010.

OWNER OF U.S. REG. NOS. 3,657,327 AND 3,724,808.

THE MARK CONSISTS OF THE LETTERS "F E V E R". THE LETTER "V" IS LARGE AND THE SECOND LETTER "E" IS BACKWARDS.

SER. NO. 85-205,670, FILED 12-26-2010.

ANDREA K. NADELMAN, EXAMINING ATTORNEY

David J. Kappos

Director of the United States Patent and Trademark Office

An example of a "Special Form Mark":

United States of America
United States Patent and Trademark Office

Reg. No. 3,724,808
Registered Dec. 15, 2009

Int. Cl.: 25

TRADEMARK
PRINCIPAL REGISTER

FOR: SHOES; SNEAKERS; WOMEN'S SHOES, IN CLASS 25 (U.S. CLS. 22 AND 39).

FIRST USE 1-1-2009; IN COMMERCE 2-14-2009.

THE MARK CONSISTS OF STYLIZED LETTERS IN THE WORD "FEVER BY NATISCHA HARVEY" WITH STARS AND DOTS ABOVE THE WORD "FEVER". WITH A STYLISH SCROLL AFTER THE STYLIZED LETTER "R" IN THE WORD "FEVER".

SER. NO. 77-682,122, FILED 3-3-2009.

ALICE BENMAMAN, EXAMINING ATTORNEY

Director of the United States Patent and Trademark Office

An example of a "Standard Character or Special Form":

United States of America
United States Patent and Trademark Office

Reg. No. 4,212,379
Registered Sep. 25, 2012
Int. Cl.: 25

TRADEMARK

PRINCIPAL REGISTER

FOR: FOOTWEAR, EXCLUDING FOOTWEAR FOR COSTUMES AND DRESS-UP, IN CLASS 25 (U.S. CLS. 22 AND 39).

FIRST USE 3-15-2011; IN COMMERCE 3-15-2011.

OWNER OF U.S. REG. NOS. 3,657,327 AND 3,724,808.

THE NAME "NATISCHA HARVEY" IDENTIFIES A LIVING INDIVIDUAL WHOSE CONSENT IS OF RECORD.

THE MARK CONSISTS OF THE WORDS "FEVER BY NATISCHA HARVEY." THE LETTER "V" IS LARGER AND THE SECOND LETTER "E" IS BACKWARDS. THE WORDING "BY NATISCHA HARVEY" IS IN CURSIVE.

SER. NO. 85-306,967, FILED 4-28-2011.

ALICIA COLLINS, EXAMINING ATTORNEY

Director of the United States Patent and Trademark Office

CHAPTER 7

Additional Business Information

When starting a business there are a lot of minor details that business owners overlook partially because they are extremely excited about the overall concept of starting the business. Business owners need to always be sure to dot their "i's" and cross their "t's", which can make or break a business. This chapter will focus on some minor things in a business that are overlooked.

Appearance

If you are not an online store or you do not sell products online, a business location would be ideal, even if it is just an office location. When charging fee's you should not charge extremely high professional rates especially if you are new and possibly meeting customers or potential clients at business locations such as Starbucks or Dunkin Doughnuts, or similar locations other than your business location. Having an actual location speaks highly of your business and your professionalism. When obtaining a business or office location be sure your actual location is open, bright, clean, smells great, is professional, and inviting. This is important because customers need to feel welcome, they need to like what they see, and they need to feel safe.

Customers

Always remember your customers are your business. Great customer service is ALWAYS key. It will bring your business more customers and retain current customers. When situations arise and you are resolving incidents with a customer, be sure to "end" on a positive note with a positive mark imbedded in the customer's mind. To engage with customers you may want to have incentive programs, contest, or a rewards program which aids in retaining customers and also makes them feel valuable.

Answering service

To receive phone calls you can always use an "answering service" that can answer your business phone calls at a specified time and in a professional manner. This prevents customers from calling you on your personal phone while still ensuring the customers are being taken care of and needs are met. You can provide specific details on what you would like said and explained to callers while professionalism is being provided. There are several companies that you can utilize for these services. If you are just starting out and do not have funding to hire an answering service you may want to set-up a free "Google" telephone number and transfer calls to your mobile phone. This way a customer can call that particular number and not your personal cell phone number.

Payments

When accepting payments you will need a merchant provider to process credit, debit, telecheck, and other forms of payment. There are several merchant providers to choose from. Just remember before selecting a merchant provider to look at their fees and pricing. You must have your business license and your EIN number prior to applying with merchant providers. Some common merchant providers that new businesses tend to use are PayPal and Square. It is important that when you start accepting credit cards that you "batch" out at the end of each business day. Meaning at the end of each business day to receive all necessary monies made for that day all sales must be cleared and accounting for, which is typically set up when you open your credit card machine or account. If it is not set up contact your credit card provider to further assist you in setting up daily batching for your company. You may also have "your batching" automatically scheduled. In regards to receiving payments, I would highly recommend not taking checks unless they are telechecks. this can save you a lot of time, money, and prevent headaches.

Refund/Exchange Policy

Be sure that you always provide and have the "Refund/Exchange Policy" visible. This is essential when customers try to return or exchange merchandise. Be sure that it is very clear and understandable. This aids in returns or disputes with your merchant provider and can help prevent any lawsuits against you or your business.

A simple Refund/Exchange Policy is located below: (Have the company logo at the top of the policy)

(Company name here) will accept exchanges of regular-priced merchandise with in 15 days of purchase. Merchandise must be unworn, in its original box, with its original tag, and accompanied with the original receipt. Merchandise that is unwashed, unworn, and not damaged may be returned for store credit or an exchange of equal value. Store Credit and Gift Cards are not redeemable for cash and cannot be replaced if lost or stolen. Sale items, accessories, and handbags are all final sale. Sale items cannot be returned or exchanged for store credit. We apologize, there are no cash refunds or a credit applied back to the card made for payment. Thank you for your Continuous Shopping here at (Company name here).

It is always a pleasure doing business with you.

A simple Refund/Exchange Policy is located below for online business:

RETURNING/EXCHANGING PURCHASED
Merchandise at (enter website here)

We pride ourselves on customer service and satisfaction. You may exchange most merchandise, less shipping charges, based on the original form of payment, unworn and original packaging within 14 days of purchase. NO EXCEPTIONS! Once your merchandise has shipped, it cannot be canceled. If you are not pleased with your purchased merchandise, you may receive a store credit ONLY within 14 days of purchase. We are not responsible for any loss or damage of any returned item(s) prior to our receipt while in transit. All orders returned after 14 days will not be accepted and will be returned to the customer at the customer's expense. If you have received an item that is damaged or defective, please contact us immediately. We will file a claim and send you a pre-paid shipping return slip for you to return the merchandise. Once we have received the items, we will immediately send out a replacement to you. If your purchased merchandise does not fit, you may exchange it for another size within 14 days, No Exceptions and you will not receive a refund. If the item/size you are exchanging is not available, you will receive a store credit and not a monetary refund. If you are returning a gift, you will receive a web merchandise credit. All items on Sale, Special, or at a Reduced Price are FINAL SALE (no returns, no exchanges)! Please remember all merchandise returned or exchanged must be in its original condition (new), and in box. Adverse weather may cause a delay in shipping. If this happens, we apologize for any delays but cannot control the weather and will not be responsible for any delays nor will any refunds on neither the cost of shipping nor the cost of a purchase be refunded.

In the case of an exchange: You will be charged for the shipment of your replacement item UNLESS there was an error on the company's behalf. For example: If the incorrect size or color was shipped. If we do not have your exchange size we will notify you via email of the next delivery date. Please write the requested size on the Sales Receipt Slip and place inside the box. Unfortunately, we do not pay for exchange shipments unless there was an error on our part. When receiving an exchange an invoice will be emailed to you for shipping or any additional charges.

Exchange (enter website here) merchandise by mail
You may ship the merchandise to: (Your companies address). Merchandise

must be received within 14 days, NO EXCEPTIONS. You will be charged for the shipment of your replacement item UNLESS there was an error on the companies' behalf. The shipping charge will be emailed to you. Once it is paid, your item will be shipped and your UPS tracking information will be emailed to you. When exchanging securely pack your merchandise with the invoice or sales receipt. Please notate the reason and size you are exchanging your merchandise for. Ship returned merchandise via UPS, FED EX, or USPS. Please insure your package and receive tracking information. We'll process your exchange within 7 days of receipt. If you provided an email address, we'll notify you via email when your exchange has been received and processed. If the requested exchange item is not available, you will receive a store credit. If you have questions or would like assistance with a return or exchange, please refer to the FAQ tab located on our website. If you have further questions or would like assistance with a return, please contact us by email at: (Your companies email address goes here).

Non-Disclosures/Non-Compete
Non-disclosure forms- if you are designing, making, creating, having a meeting, or have items that you want to remain private, a non-disclosure agreement between the parties should be signed. With a non-disclosure agreement, all information will and shall remain confidential. Once signed, disclosing any information would be in violation of the disclosure and legal ramifications can apply. A non-compete agreement, is typically provided to the employees of your establishment at the time they are hired outlining details of what may not occur and what can not be done when they no longer are employed by you. The agreement explains in detail that when the employee is no longer employed by your company they can not work within the same field or with a competitor in "x" amount of years. They are not allowed to compete with your business or become your competition. A detailed example of a non-disclosure is located in Chapter 8.

To set up your own companies Non-Disclosure Agreement you would have your companies name at the top of the paper and include similar information in your agreement:

This Nondisclosure Agreement (the "Agreement") is entered into by **(Your Company Name here)**, and **(Enter opposing party/person/company)** with its principal offices at, **(Your Company Address here) and (Enter opposing party/person/company address)** for the purpose of preventing the unauthorized disclosure of Confidential Information as defined below. The parties agree to enter into a confidential relationship with respect to the disclosure of all designs given by **(Your Company Name here)**, and certain proprietary and confidential information including all designs and logos in there entirety ("Confidential Information").

1. Definition of Confidential Information. For purposes of this Agreement, "Confidential Information" shall include all information or material that has or could have commercial value or other utility in the business in which Disclosing Party is engaged. If Confidential Information is in written form, the Disclosing Party shall label or stamp the materials with the word "Confidential" or some similar warning. If Confidential Information is transmitted orally, the Disclosing Party shall promptly provide a writing indicating that such oral communication constituted Confidential Information. Confidential also meaning to never: disclose, sale, copy, reveal, alter, share, nor show any designs created by **(Your Company Name here)**, to anyone other than **(Your Company Name here)**, staff and members or you shall be prosecuted to the fullest existent of the law. All designs created by **(Your Company Name here)**, shall remain property of **(Your Company Name here)**,

2. Exclusions from Confidential Information. Receiving Party's obligations under this Agreement does not extend to information that is: (a) publicly known at the time of disclosure or subsequently becomes publicly known through no fault of the Receiving Party; (b) discovered or created by the Receiving Party before disclosure by Disclosing Party; (c) learned by the Receiving Party through legitimate means other than from the Disclosing Party or Disclosing Party's representatives; or (d) is disclosed by Receiving Party with Disclosing Party's prior written approval.

3. Obligations of Receiving Party. Receiving Party shall hold and maintain the Confidential Information in strictest confidence for the sole and exclusive benefit of the Disclosing Party. Receiving Party shall carefully restrict access to Confidential Information to employees, contractors and third parties as is reasonably required and shall require those persons to sign nondisclosure restrictions at least as protective as those in this Agreement. Receiving Party shall not, without prior written approval of Disclosing Party, use for Receiving Party's own benefit, publish, copy, or otherwise disclose to others, or permit the use by others for their benefit or to the detriment of Disclosing Party, any Confidential Information. Receiving Party shall return to Disclosing Party any and all records, notes, and other written, printed, or tangible materials in its possession pertaining to Confidential Information immediately if Disclosing Party requests it in writing.

4. Time Periods. The nondisclosure provisions of this Agreement shall survive the termination of this Agreement and Receiving Party's duty to hold Confidential Information in confidence shall remain in effect until the Confidential Information no longer qualifies as a trade secret or until Disclosing Party sends Receiving Party written notice releasing Receiving Party from this Agreement, whichever occurs first.

5. Relationships. Nothing contained in this Agreement shall be deemed to constitute either party a partner, joint venturer or employee of the other party for any purpose.

6. Severability. If a court finds any provision of this Agreement invalid or unenforceable, the remainder of this Agreement shall be interpreted so as best to effect the intent of the parties.

7. Integration. This Agreement expresses the complete understanding of the parties with respect to the subject matter and supersedes all prior proposals, agreements, representations and understandings. This Agreement may not be amended except in a writing signed by both parties.

8. Waiver. The failure to exercise any right provided in this Agreement shall not be a waiver of prior or subsequent rights.

This Agreement and each party's obligations shall be binding on the representatives, assigns, and successors of such party. Each party has signed this Agreement through its authorized representative.

Authorized Signature
(Typed or Print Name)
Date:

Authorized Signature
(Typed or Print Name)
Date:

Consent Form

If you are using images or anything that doesn't belong to you or your business for marketing or promotions, a consent form should be signed by both you and the individuals or their representative which allows your company to use the images. For example, images of a model for your website, store window, or marketing materials. A consent form should be signed by the individuals, companies, or parties so that no legal ramifications may occur in the future and it allows you to use the image.

Disclaimer for online websites

We are all human and we all make mistakes. If you own an online store a disclaimer is needed for any errors. An example is: (Your company name goes here) tries to ensure that listed prices are accurate. Occasionally, due to human error or otherwise, an incorrect price is or maybe listed. We are not responsible for erroneously listed, printed prices or other typographical errors that may occur.

Hiring Employees

When first starting out most businesses do not have a Human Resource Department or a large staff. In business you always want to remain professional and have a professional working environment so a tone needs to be set for your business. You should conduct a professional interview and always check potential employee references. When employees are hired and before they start provide employees with an employee handbook, offer of employment contract, and a non-compete disclosure. Examples of some of these are located in Chapter 8.

The handbook should outline all the rules, regulations, and expectations of your business and their job. Be sure that it is signed by new employees, which signifies they actually received and read the handbook. An example of an employee handbook is located in Chapter 8.

Before the new employee starts work an offer of employment contract should be provided which includes the employee's position title, their start date, the current manager, their compensation, their benefits if any, and the terms of employment. The terms of employment should outline the

1. Position and Duties
2. The outside Business Activities
3. Employment Classification
4. Compensation/Benefits.

The Compensation/Benefits should be broken down and detailed. It should include the employees wage, their reimbursement of expenses, their withholdings and their benefits. It should also include an "At-Will Employment", meaning they can be terminated at anytime. A non-disclosure agreement or non-compete should be included as well meaning they can not disclose any information in regards to your business nor can they become your competitor or work with another company in the same line of work within a number of years. An "Offer of Employment Contract" example is located in Chapter 8.

When hiring employees a payroll company can be hired to conduct all payroll and employee information regarding pay unless the employees are contracted, in which taxes would be their responsibility. If they are contracted the business must supply them with a 1099 so taxes can be filed on both your company and they can file them as well. If an employee is hired they would need to provide you with a copy of their card holders government officiated identification, social security card/information, and a completed W-2. A form would need to be completed by the new employee, which would include the general basic information as well as the following: hire date; rehire date, separation date, or change date, pay type: W2, 1099, or 3rd party, social security or 1099 EIN, federal withholding, pay frequencies, pay type, salary, unemployment state and withholding state, and other basic information. You should also have your new employee sign an "Acknowledgement of Stealing Merchandise". This is to let employees know that if any theft occurs they may be prosecuted to the fullest extent of the law. A simple "Acknowledgement of Stealing Merchandise" example is located in Chapter 8. Be sure to also have the rules, regulations, and "Fire at Will" outlined and make sure they sign this which would be confirming that they have received, reviewed, and understood your companies policies, rules, and regulations.

Employee Hand Book
An employee handbook needs to be provided to all employees when hired. The handbook needs to be signed acknowledging that they received a copy of the handbook and that they understood it in its entirety. The handbook should include:

A welcome letter, the company's history, mission, obligations, equal employment opportunity, drug and alcohol policy, open door policy, employee classifications, introductory period, hours of work, personnel record, reporting changes in personal information, release of pay checks, on-he-job- solicitation/distribution, general information such as absences, bulletin boards, parking facilities, personal appearance, safety, telephone calls, workers compensation, moving up which includes promotion and advancement opportunities, wages and rates of pay, employee participation, communication, suggestions, complainant and grievance procedure. It should also place emphasis on corrective discipline, leaves of absence (family and medical leave, maternity leave, military leave, and personal leave), employee benefits (holidays, vacation, sick leave, insurance plus, 401k retirement plan, employee purchasing discounts, bereavement pay, jury duty leave, and leaving employment (final pay check, job abandonment, re-employment). An example of an employee handbook is located in Chapter 8.

When starting out your company's handbook may not be anywhere near this detailed so do not feel intimated but it does need to be as specific as possible. Have a clause in the handbook that states, "This is written by my personal experiences and views and is not subject to any laws but is strictly (your companies name) policy, rules, and regulations. Or something similar. Be sure that each employee receives a handbook and signs an "Acknowledgment of Handbook" acknowledging that they received, read, and understood everything inside. This way the employees are completely aware of what is required, expected, and accepted in your companies working environment. Examples of both, "Acknowledgement of Handbook" and "Employee Hand Book" are located in Chapter 8.

Remember

A lot goes into owning your own business, which I am certain you are aware. There are some common yet minor things that are overlooked when starting a business. For example, purchasing insurance. You should purchase insurance for the company, location, items pertaining to the business, individuals at your location, and the merchandise. Another thing to remember is filing the business returns be it sales tax or quarterly returns, even if there is nothing to report. Please also remember to retain all documents pertaining to your business and receipts as this is important for filing taxes, knowing the growth in your company, or for auditing purposes. Also always be mindful that your business license needs to be renewed yearly as well as your filings with the Secretary of State. When picking a location for the business know that location is key and it is vital to your business. Also know that seeking assistance is a great thing, you are only one person, and can only do so much. If you need assistance you may want to look into a marketing, social media, and/or public relations team. These teams may be able to aid in exposure for the business and/or expansion in the company.

Remember in your business everything you go through grows you. What you put into it, is what you will get out of it. Never give up and always focus on the larger picture. Know that with owning your own business comes responsibility. You must worry less and have faith that things will work out the way they are suppose to. Congratulations on all your business endeavors, wishing you much success, now get to work!

"There are many things in life that will catch your eye, but only a few will catch your heart. Pursue these."

-Michael Nolan

CHAPTER 8

Example of Forms

An example of an "Acknowledgement of Stealing Merchandise":

Logo Here

Acknowledgment of Stealing Merchandise

This letter is for the sole purpose of theft, if there is any theft in, dealing, with or associated with (your company name here), you will be prosecuted to the fullest extent of the law.

Employees Name (printed): _____

Employees Signature: _____

Date: _____

An example of a "Non-Discloser Agreement":

LOGO HERE

Fever Nondisclosure Agreement

This Nondisclosure Agreement (the "Agreement") is entered into by (Company Name) with its principal offices at (Address) and (Opposing Party Name) located at (Opposing Party Address) for the purpose of preventing the unauthorized disclosure of Confidential Information as defined below. The parties agree to enter into a confidential relationship with respect to the disclosure of all designs given by (Company Name), and certain proprietary and confidential information including all designs and logos in there entirety ("Confidential Information").

1. Definition of Confidential Information. For purposes of this Agreement, "Confidential Information" shall include all information or material that has or could have commercial value or other utility in the business in which Disclosing Party is engaged. If Confidential Information is in written form, the Disclosing Party shall label or stamp the materials with the word "Confidential" or some similar warning. If Confidential Information is transmitted orally, the Disclosing Party shall promptly provide a writing indicating that such oral communication constituted Confidential Information. Confidential also meaning to never: disclose, sale, copy, reveal, alter, share, nor show any designs created by (Company Name) to anyone other than (Company Name) staff and members or you shall be prosecuted to the fullest existent of the law. All designs created by (Company Name) shall remain property of (Company Name).

2. Exclusions from Confidential Information. Receiving Party's obligations under this Agreement do not extend to information that is: (a) publicly known at the time of disclosure or subsequently becomes publicly known through no fault of the Receiving Party; (b) discovered or created by the Receiving Party before disclosure by Disclosing Party; (c) learned by the Receiving Party through legitimate means other than from the Disclosing Party or Disclosing Party's representatives; or (d) is disclosed by Receiving Party with Disclosing Party's prior written approval.

3. Obligations of Receiving Party. Receiving Party shall hold and maintain the Confidential Information in strictest confidence for the sole and exclusive benefit of the Disclosing Party. Receiving Party shall carefully restrict access to Confidential Information to employees, contractors and third parties as is reasonably required and shall require those persons to sign nondisclosure restrictions at least as protective as those in this Agreement. Receiving Party shall not, without prior written approval of Disclosing Party, use for Receiving Party's own benefit, publish, copy, or otherwise disclose to others, or permit the use by others for their benefit or to the detriment of Disclosing Party, any Confidential Information. Receiving Party shall return to Disclosing Party any and all records, notes, and other written, printed, or tangible materials in its possession pertaining to Confidential Information immediately if Disclosing Party requests it in writing.

4. Time Periods. The nondisclosure provisions of this Agreement shall survive the termination of this Agreement and Receiving Party's duty to hold Confidential Information in confidence shall remain in effect until the Confidential Information no longer qualifies as a trade secret or until Disclosing Party sends Receiving Party written notice releasing Receiving Party from this Agreement, whichever occurs first.

5. Relationships. Nothing contained in this Agreement shall be deemed to constitute either party a partner, joint venturer or employee of the other party for any purpose.

6. Severability. If a court finds any provision of this Agreement invalid or unenforceable, the remainder of this Agreement shall be interpreted so as best to effect the intent of the parties.

7. Integration. This Agreement expresses the complete understanding of the parties with respect to the subject matter and supersedes all prior proposals, agreements, representations and understandings. This Agreement may not be amended except in a writing signed by both parties.

8. Waiver. The failure to exercise any right provided in this Agreement shall not be a waiver of prior or subsequent rights.

This Agreement and each party's obligations shall be binding on the representatives, assigns and successors of such party. Each party has signed this Agreement through its authorized representative.

Authorized Signature: _____

(Typed or Printed Name) (Your Company Name): _____

Date: _____

Authorized Signature: _____

(Typed or Printed Name) (Opposing Party Name): _____

Date: _____

An example of an "Acknowledgement of Receipt of Employee Handbook":

LOGO HERE

Acknowledgment of Receipt of Employee Handbook

The Employee Handbook describes important information about (Your Company Name), and I understand that I should consult the Human Resources Department regarding any questions not answered in the Employee Handbook.

Since the information, policies, and benefits described here are necessarily subject to change, I acknowledge that revisions to the Employee Handbook may occur. All such changes will be communicated through official notices. I understand that revised information may supersede, modify, or eliminate existing policies.

Furthermore, I acknowledge that this Employee Handbook is neither a contract of employment nor a legal document. I have received the Employee Handbook and I understand that it is my responsibility to read and comply with the policies contained in this Employee Handbook and any revisions made to it.

Employee's Name (printed): _____

Employee's Signature: _____

Date: _____

An example of an "Application for Employment- Long Form":

LOGO HERE

Application for Employment-Long Form//

Our policy is to provide equal employment opportunity to all qualified persons without regard to race, creed, color, religious belief, sex, age, national origin, ancestry, physical or mental disability, or veteran status.

Our policy is to provide equal employment opportunity to all qualified persons without regard to race, creed, color, religious belief, sex, age, national origin, ancestry, physical or mental disability, or veteran status.

Name

Last _____ First _____

Middle_____

Date _____

Street Address

_____

City _____ State _____ ZIP _____

Telephone _____

Social Security # _____

Position applied for _____

How did you hear of this opening?

_____

When can you start? _____ Desired Wage

$_____

Are you a U.S. citizen or otherwise authorized to work in the U.S. on an unrestricted basis? (You may be required to provide documentation.) ❑ Yes ❑ No

Are you looking for full-time employment? ❑ Yes ❑ No

If no, what hours are you available? _____

Are you willing to work swing shift? ❑ Yes ❑ No

Are you willing to work graveyard? ❑ Yes ❑ No

Have you ever been convicted of a felony? (This will not necessarily affect your application.)

❑ Yes ❑ No

If yes, please describe conditions.

_____

Employment Desired

Have you ever applied for employment here? ❑ Yes ❑ No

When? _____

Where?_____

Have you ever been employed by (Your Company Name)? ❑ Yes ❑ No

When? _____

Where?_____

Are you presently employed? ❑ Yes ❑ No

May we contact your present employer? ❑ Yes ❑ No

Are you available for full-time work? ❑ Yes ❑ No

Are you available for part-time work? ❑ Yes ❑ No

Will you relocate? ❑ Yes ❑ No

Are you willing to travel? ❑ Yes ❑ No If yes, what percent?

_____

Date you can
start_____

Desired
position_____

Desired starting
salary_____

Please list applicable
skills_____

Education:	School Name and Location	Year	Major
Degree			
High School _____		_____	_____
College _____		_____	_____
College _____		_____	_____
Post-College _____		_____	_____
Other Training _____		_____	_____

In addition to your work history, are there are other skills, qualifications, or experience that we should consider?

_____

Please list any scholastic honors received and offices held in school.

_____

Are you planning to continue your studies? ❑ Yes ❑ No

If yes, where and what courses of study?

_____

Company Name

_____

Address _____Telephone _____

Date Started _____ Starting Wage _____ Starting Position

Date Ended _____ Ending Wage _____ Ending Position

Name of Supervisor _____

May we contact? ❑ Yes ❑ No

Responsibilities

_____

Reason for leaving

_____

Company Name
_____

Address _____ Telephone _____
Date Started _____ Starting Wage _____ Starting Position
Date Ended _____ Ending Wage _____ Ending Position
Name of Supervisor _____
May we contact? ❑ Yes ❑ No
Responsibilities
_____

Reason for leaving
_____

Company Name
_____

Address _____ Telephone _____
Date Started _____ Starting Wage _____ Starting Position
_____

Date Ended _____ Ending Wage _____ Ending Position
_____

Name of Supervisor _____
May we contact? ❑ Yes ❑ No
Responsibilities
_____

Reason for leaving
_____

Company Name
_____

Address _____ Telephone
_____

Date Started _____ Starting Wage _____ Starting Position
Date Ended _____ Ending Wage _____ Ending Position
References
List three personal references, not related to you, who have known you for more than one year.
Name _____ Phone _____Years Known_____
Address
_____

Name _____ Phone _____Years Known_____
Address
_____

Name _____ Phone _____Years Known_____
Address
_____

Emergency Contact
In case of emergency, please
notify:_____
Name _____ Phone _____

Address
_____
Name _____ Phone _____
Address

_____

Please Read Before Signing:

I certify that all information provided by me on this application is true and complete to the best of my knowledge and that I have withheld nothing that, if disclosed, would alter the integrity of this application.

I authorize my previous employers, schools, or persons listed as references to give any information regarding employment or educational record. I agree that (Your Company Name) and my previous employers will not be held liable in any respect if a job offer is not extended, or is withdrawn, or employment is terminated because of false statements, omissions, or answers made by myself on this application. In the event of any employment with (Your Company Name), I will comply with all rules and regulations as set by the company in any communication distributed to the employees.

In compliance with the Immigration Reform and Control Act of 1986, I understand that I am required to provide approved documentation to the company that verifies my right to work in the United States on the first day of employment. I have received from the company a list of the approved documents that are required.

I understand that employment at (Your Company Name) is "at will," which means that either I or (Your Company Name) can terminate the employment relationship at any time, with or without prior notice, and for any reason not prohibited by statute. All employment is continued on that basis. I hereby acknowledge that I have read and understand the above statements.

Signature _____ Date_____

Immigration Reform and Control Act Requirement

In compliance with the Immigration Reform and Control Act of 1986, you are required to provide approved documentation that verifies your right to work in the United States prior to your employment with (Your Company Name). Please be prepared to provide us with the following documentation in the event you are offered and accept employment with our company.

Any one of the following: (These establish both identity and employment authorization.)

1. U.S. Passport.
2. Certificate of U.S. Citizenship (issued by USCIS).
3. Certificate of Naturalization (issued by USCIS).
4. Resident alien card or other alien unexpired endorsement card, with photo or other approved identifying information which evidences employment authorization.
5. Unexpired foreign passport with unexpired endorsement authorizing employment.

Or one from List A and List B:

List A (These establish employment authorization.)
1.   Social Security card.
2.   Birth Certificate or other documentation that establishes U.S. nationality or birth.
3.   Other approved documentation.

List B
1.   Driver's license or similar government identification card with photo or other approved identifying information.
2.   Other approved documentation of identity for applicants under age 16 or in a state that does not issue an I.D. card (other than a driver's license).

An example of an "Application for Employment- Short Form":

LOGO HERE

Application for Employment—Short Form

Our policy is to provide equal employment opportunity to all qualified persons without regard to race, creed, color, religious belief, sex, age, national origin, ancestry, physical or mental disability, or veteran status.

Name

Last _____ First _____

Middle_____

Date _____

Street Address

_____

City _____ State _____ ZIP _____

Telephone _____

Social Security # _____

Position applied for _____

How did you hear of this opening?

_____

When can you start? _____ Desired Wage

$_____

Are you a U.S. citizen or otherwise authorized to work in the U.S. on an unrestricted basis? (You may be required to provide documentation.) ❑ Yes ❑ No

Are you looking for full-time employment? ❑ Yes ❑ No

If no, what hours are you available? _____

Are you willing to work swing shift? ❑ Yes ❑ No

Are you willing to work graveyard? ❑ Yes ❑ No

Have you ever been convicted of a felony? (This will not necessarily affect your application.) ❑ Yes ❑ No

If yes, please describe conditions.

_____

Education School Name and Location	Year	Major
Degree		
High School _____	_____	_____
College _____	_____	_____
College _____	_____	_____
Post-College _____	_____	_____
Other Training _____	_____	_____

In addition to your work history, are there other skills, qualifications, or experience that we should consider?

_____

Employment History   (Start with most recent employer)
Company Name

_____

Address _____ Telephone _____

Date Started _____ Starting Wage _____ Starting Position

Date Ended _____ Ending Wage _____ Ending Position

Name of Supervisor _____

May we contact? ❑ Yes ❑ No

Responsibilities

_____

Company Name

_____

Address _____ Telephone

_____

Date Started _____ Starting Wage _____ Starting Position

_____

Date Ended _____ Ending Wage _____ Ending Position

_____

Name of Supervisor _____

May we contact? ❑ Yes ❑ No

Responsibilities

_____

Reason for leaving

_____

Company Name

_____

Address _____ Telephone _____

Date Started _____ Starting Wage _____ Starting Position

Date Ended _____ Ending Wage _____ Ending Position

Name of Supervisor _____

May we contact? ❑ Yes ❑ No

Responsibilities

_____

_____

Reason for leaving

_____

Company Name

_____

Address _____ Telephone _____

Date Started _____ Starting Wage _____ Starting Position

Date Ended _____ Ending Wage _____ Ending Position

Name of Supervisor _____

May we contact? ❑ Yes ❑ No

Responsibilities

_____

Reason for leaving

_____

Attach additional information if necessary.

I certify that the facts set forth in this application for employment are true and complete to the best of my knowledge. I understand that if I am employed, false statements on this application shall be considered sufficient cause for dismissal. (Your Company Name) is hereby authorized to make any investigations of my prior educational and employment history.

I understand that employment at (Your Company Name) is "at will," which means that either I or (Your Company Name) can terminate the employment relationship at any time, with or without prior notice, and for any reason not prohibited by statute. All employment is continued on that basis. I understand that no supervisor, manager, or executive of (Your Company Name), other than the president, has any authority to alter the foregoing.

Signature_____   Date _____

An example of an "Employee Handbook":

<u>LOGO HERE</u>

<u>(Your Company Name) Employee Handbook</u>

(Your Company Name) Employee Handbook

Issue Date:

Version Number: ___

To _____ (Employee's Name):

This is our new Employee Handbook. Please review it and sign the attached acknowledgment.

You may keep a copy of the Handbook if you wish, but a copy will always be available to you through the HR department. If you do not wish to keep a copy, please return the Handbook to HR.

This Employee Handbook (the "Handbook") was developed to describe some of the expectations of our employees and to outline the policies, programs, and benefits available to eligible employees. Employees should familiarize themselves with the contents of the Handbook as soon as possible, for it will answer many questions about employment with (Your Company Name) INTRODUCTORY STATEMENT

This Handbook is designed to acquaint you with (YOUR COMPANY NAME) and provide you with information about working conditions, employee benefits, and some of the policies affecting your employment. This Handbook is not a contract and is not intended to create any contractual or legal obligations. You should read, understand, and comply with all provisions of the Handbook. It describes many of your responsibilities as an employee and outlines the programs developed by (YOUR COMPANY NAME) to benefit employees. One of our objectives is to provide a work environment that is conducive to both personal and professional growth.

No Handbook can anticipate every circumstance or question about policy. As (YOUR COMPANY NAME) continues to grow, the need may arise and (YOUR COMPANY NAME) reserves the right to revise, supplement, or rescind any policies or portion of the Handbook from time to time as it deems appropriate, in its sole and absolute discretion. The only exception is our employment-at-will policy permitting you or (YOUR COMPANY NAME) to end our relationship for any reason at any time. The employment-at-will policy cannot be changed except in a written agreement signed by both you and the President of (YOUR COMPANY NAME) Employees will, of course, be notified of such changes to the Handbook as they occur.

Customers are among our organization's most valuable assets. Every employee represents (YOUR COMPANY NAME) to our customers and the public. The way we do our jobs presents an image of our entire organization. Customers judge all of us by how they are treated with each employee contact. Therefore, one of our first business priorities is to assist any customer or potential customer. Nothing is more important than being courteous, friendly, helpful, and prompt in the attention you give to customers.

(YOUR COMPANY NAME) will provide customer relations and services training to all employees with extensive customer contact. Our personal contact with the public, our manners on the telephone, and the communications we send to customers are a reflection not only of ourselves, but also of the professionalism of (YOUR COMPANY NAME). Positive customer relations not only enhance the public's perception or image of (YOUR COMPANY NAME), but also pay off in greater customer loyalty and increased sales and profit. All information, opportunities, advances, benefits, and compensations may vary and vary depending on each employee, there job title and there job descriptions, as well as roles with (YOUR COMPANY NAME)

1-01 Nature of Employment

Employment with (YOUR COMPANY NAME) is voluntarily entered into and is "at-will," which means that the employee is free to resign at will at any time, with notice and cause. Similarly, (YOUR COMPANY NAME) may terminate the employment relationship at any time, with or without notice or cause, so long as there is no violation of applicable federal or state law. No one has the authority to make verbal statements that change the at-will nature of employment, and the at-will relationship cannot be changed or modified for any employee except in a written agreement signed by that employee and the President of (YOUR COMPANY NAME).

Policies set forth in this Handbook are not intended to create a contract, nor are they to be construed to constitute contractual obligations of any kind or a contract of employment between (YOUR COMPANY NAME) and any of its employees. The provisions of the Handbook have been developed at the discretion of management and, except for its policy of employment-at-will, may be amended or cancelled at any time, at (YOUR COMPANY NAME) 's sole discretion.

These provisions supersede all existing policies and practices and may not be amended or added to without the express written approval of the CEO or person designated by the CEO of (YOUR COMPANY NAME)

1-02 Employee Relations

(YOUR COMPANY NAME) believes that the work conditions, wages, and benefits it offers to its employees are competitive with those offered by other employers in this area and in this industry. If employees have concerns about work conditions or compensation, they are strongly encouraged to voice these concerns openly and directly to their supervisors.

Our experience has shown that when employees deal openly and directly with supervisors, the work environment can be excellent, communications can be clear, and attitudes can be positive. We believe that (YOUR COMPANY NAME) amply demonstrates its commitment to employees by responding effectively to employee concerns.

1-03 Equal Employment Opportunity

In order to provide equal employment and advancement opportunities to all individuals, employment decisions at (YOUR COMPANY NAME) will be based on merit, qualifications, and the needs of (YOUR COMPANY NAME). (YOUR COMPANY NAME) does not unlawfully discriminate in employment opportunities or practices on the basis of race, color, religion, sex, national origin, age, disability, ancestry, medical conditions, family care status, sexual orientation, or any other basis prohibited by law.

(YOUR COMPANY NAME) will make reasonable accommodations for qualified individuals with known disabilities unless doing so would result in an undue hardship to the extent required by law. This policy governs all aspects of employment, including selection, job assignment, compensation, discipline, termination, and access to benefits and training.

Any employees with questions or concerns about any type of discrimination in the workplace are encouraged to bring these issues to the attention of their immediate supervisor or the Human Resources Department. Employees can raise concerns and make reports without fear of reprisal. Anyone found to be engaging in any type of unlawful discrimination will be subject to disciplinary action, up to and including termination of employment.

1-04 Business Ethics and Conduct

The successful business operation and reputation of (YOUR COMPANY NAME) are built upon the principles of fair dealing and ethical conduct of our employees. Our reputation for integrity and excellence requires careful observance of the spirit and the letter of all applicable laws and regulations, as well as a scrupulous regard for the highest standards of conduct and personal integrity.

The continued success of (YOUR COMPANY NAME) is dependent upon our customers' trust and we are dedicated to preserving that trust. Employees owe a duty to (YOUR COMPANY NAME), its customers, and its shareholders to act in a way that will merit the continued trust and confidence of the public.

(YOUR COMPANY NAME) will comply with all applicable laws and regulations and expects its directors, officers, and employees to conduct business in accordance with the letter, spirit, and intent of all relevant laws and to refrain from any illegal, dishonest, or unethical conduct.

In general, the use of good judgment, based on high ethical principles, will guide you with respect to lines of acceptable conduct. If a situation arises where it is difficult to determine the proper course of action, the matter should be discussed openly with your immediate supervisor and, if necessary, with the Human Resources Department for advice and consultation.

Compliance with this policy of business ethics and conduct is the responsibility of every (YOUR COMPANY NAME) employee. Disregarding or failing to comply with this standard of business ethics and conduct could lead to disciplinary action, up to and including possible termination of employment.

1-05 Personal Relationships in the Workplace

The employment of relatives or individuals involved in a dating relationship in the same area of an organization may cause serious conflicts and problems with favoritism and employee morale. In addition to claims of partiality in treatment at work, personal conflicts from outside the work environment can be carried over into day-to-day working relationships.

For purposes of this policy, relatives are any persons who are related to each other by blood or marriage or whose relationship is similar to that of persons who are related by blood or marriage. A dating relationship is defined as a relationship that may be reasonably expected to lead to the formation of a consensual "romantic" or sexual relationship. This policy applies to all employees without regard to the gender or sexual orientation of the individuals involved.

Relatives of current employees may not occupy a position that will be working directly for or supervising their relative except as required by law. Individuals involved in a dating relationship with a current employee may also not occupy a position that will be working directly for or supervising the employee with whom they are involved in a dating relationship. (YOUR COMPANY NAME) also reserves the right to take prompt action if an actual or potential conflict of interest arises involving relatives or individuals involved in a dating relationship who occupy positions at any level (higher or lower) in the same line of authority that may affect the review of employment decisions.

If a relative relationship or dating relationship is established after employment between employees who are in a reporting situation described above, it is the responsibility and obligation of the supervisor involved in the relationship to disclose the existence of the relationship to management.

In other cases where a conflict or the potential for conflict arises because of the relationship between employees, even if there is no line of authority or reporting involved, the employees may be separated by reassignment or terminated from employment. Employees in a close personal relationship should refrain from public workplace displays of affection or excessive personal conversation.

1-07 Immigration Law Compliance

(YOUR COMPANY NAME) is committed to employing only United States citizens and aliens who are authorized to work in the United States and does not unlawfully discriminate on the basis of citizenship or national origin.

In compliance with the Immigration Reform and Control Act of 1986, each new employee, as a condition of employment, must complete the Employment Eligibility Verification Form I-9 and present documentation establishing identity and employment eligibility. Former employees who are rehired must also complete the form if they have not completed an I-9 with (YOUR COMPANY NAME) within the past three years or if their previous I-9 is no longer retained or valid.

Employees with questions or seeking more information on immigration law issues are encouraged to contact the Human Resources Department. Employees may raise questions or complaints about immigration law compliance without fear of reprisal.

1-08 Conflicts of Interest

Employees have an obligation to conduct business within guidelines that prohibit actual or potential conflicts of interest. This policy establishes only the framework within which (YOUR COMPANY NAME) wishes the business to operate. The purpose of these guidelines is to provide general direction so that employees can seek further clarification on issues related to the subject of acceptable standards of operation. Contact the Human Resources Department for more information or questions about conflicts of interest.

An actual or potential conflict of interest occurs when an employee is in a position to influence a decision that may result in a personal gain for that employee or for a relative as a result of (YOUR COMPANY NAME) 's business dealings. For the purposes of this policy, a relative is any person who is related by blood or marriage or whose relationship with the employee is similar to that of persons who are related by blood or marriage.

No "presumption of guilt" is created by the mere existence of a relationship with outside firms. However, if employees have any influence on transactions involving purchases, contracts, or leases, it is imperative that they disclose to an officer of (YOUR COMPANY NAME) as soon as possible the existence of any actual or potential conflict of interest so that safeguards can be established to protect all parties.

Personal gain may result not only in cases where an employee or relative has a significant ownership in a firm with which (YOUR COMPANY NAME) does business, but also when an employee or relative receives any kickback, bribe, substantial gift, or special consideration as a result of any transaction or business dealings involving (YOUR COMPANY NAME).

1-12 Non-Disclosure

The protection of confidential business information and trade secrets is vital to the interests and the success of (YOUR COMPANY NAME). Such confidential information includes, but is not limited to, the following examples:

- Acquisitions
- Compensation data
- Computer processes
- Computer programs and codes
- Customer lists
- Customer preferences
- Financial information
- Investments
- Labor relations strategies
- Marketing strategies
- New materials research
- Partnerships
- Pending projects and proposals
- Proprietary production processes
- Research and development strategies
- Scientific data
- Scientific formulae
- Scientific prototypes
- Technological data
- Technological prototypes

All employees may be required to sign a non-disclosure agreement as a condition of employment. Employees who improperly use or disclose trade secrets or confidential business information will be subject to disciplinary action, up to and including termination of employment and legal action, even if they do not actually benefit from the disclosed information.

1-14 Disability Accommodation

(YOUR COMPANY NAME) is committed to complying fully with applicable disability laws and ensuring equal opportunity in employment for qualified persons with disabilities.

Hiring procedures have been reviewed and provide persons with disabilities meaningful employment opportunities. Pre-employment inquiries are made regarding only an applicant's ability to perform the duties of the position.

Reasonable accommodation is available to all disabled employees, where their disability affects the performance of job functions to the extent required by law. All employment decisions are based on the merits of the situation and the needs of the (YOUR COMPANY NAME), not the disability of the individual.

(YOUR COMPANY NAME) is also committed to not unlawfully discriminating against any qualified employees or applicants because they are related to or associated with a person with a disability.

This policy is neither exhaustive nor exclusive. (YOUR COMPANY NAME) is committed to taking all other actions necessary to ensure equal employment opportunity for persons with disabilities in accordance with the ADA and all other applicable federal, state, and local laws.

2-01 Employment Categories

It is the intent of (YOUR COMPANY NAME) to clarify the definitions of employment classifications so that employees understand their employment status and benefit eligibility. These classifications do not guarantee employment for any specified period of time. Accordingly, the right to terminate the employment relationship at will at any time is retained by both the employee and (YOUR COMPANY NAME)

Each employee is designated as either NONEXEMPT or EXEMPT from federal and state wage and hour laws. NONEXEMPT employees are entitled to overtime pay under the specific provisions of federal and state laws. EXEMPT employees are excluded from specific provisions of federal and state wage and hour laws. An employee's EXEMPT or NONEXEMPT classification may be changed only upon written notification by (YOUR COMPANY NAME) management.

In addition to the above categories, each employee will belong to one other employment category:

REGULAR FULL-TIME employees are those who are not in a temporary or introductory status and who are regularly scheduled to work (YOUR COMPANY NAME) 's full-time schedule. Generally, they are eligible for (YOUR COMPANY NAME) 's benefit package, subject to the terms, conditions, and limitations of each benefit program, if decided upon hiring.

INTRODUCTORY employees are those whose performance is being evaluated to determine whether further employment in a specific position or with (YOUR COMPANY NAME) is appropriate. Employees who satisfactorily complete the introductory period will be notified of their new employment classification.

TEMPORARY employees are those who are hired as interim replacements, to temporarily supplement the work force, or to assist in the completion of a specific project. Employment assignments in this category are of a limited duration. Employment beyond any initially stated period does not in any way imply a change in employment status. Temporary employees retain that status unless and until notified of a change. While temporary employees receive all legally mandated benefits (such as workers' compensation insurance and Social Security), they are ineligible for all of (YOUR COMPANY NAME) 's other benefit programs.

2-02 Access to Personnel Files

(YOUR COMPANY NAME) maintains a personnel file on each employee. The personnel file includes such information as the employee's job application, résumé, records of training, documentation of performance appraisals and salary increases, and other employment records.

Personnel files are the property of (YOUR COMPANY NAME) and access to the information they contain is restricted. Generally, only supervisors and management personnel of (YOUR COMPANY NAME) who have a legitimate reason to review information in a file are allowed to do so.

Employees who wish to review their own file should contact the Human Resources Department. With reasonable advance notice, employees may review their own personnel files in (YOUR COMPANY NAME) 's offices and in the presence of an individual appointed by (YOUR COMPANY NAME) to maintain the files.

2-04 Personal Data Changes

It is the responsibility of each employee to promptly notify (YOUR COMPANY NAME) of any changes in personal data. Personal mailing addresses, telephone numbers, number and names of dependents, individuals to be contacted in the event of an emergency, educational accomplishments, and other such status reports should be accurate and current at all times. If any personal data has changed, notify the Human Resources Department.

2-05 Introductory Period

The introductory period is intended to give new employees the opportunity to demonstrate their ability to achieve a satisfactory level of performance and to determine whether the new position meets their expectations. (YOUR

COMPANY NAME) uses this period to evaluate employee capabilities, work habits, and overall performance. Either the employee or (YOUR COMPANY NAME) may end the employment relationship at will at any time during or after the introductory period, with or without cause or advance notice.

All new and rehired employees work on an introductory basis for the first 90 calendar days after their date of hire. Any significant absence will automatically extend an introductory period by the length of the absence. If (YOUR COMPANY NAME) determines that the designated introductory period does not allow sufficient time to thoroughly evaluate the employee's performance, the introductory period may be extended for a specified period.

2-08 Employment Applications

(YOUR COMPANY NAME) relies upon the accuracy of information contained in the employment application, as well as the accuracy of other data presented throughout the hiring process and employment. Any misrepresentations, falsifications, or material omissions in any of this information or data may result in the exclusion of the individual from further consideration for employment or, if the person has been hired, termination of employment.

In processing employment applications, (YOUR COMPANY NAME) may obtain a consumer credit report or background check for employment. If (YOUR COMPANY NAME) takes an adverse employment action based in whole or in part on any report caused by the Fair Credit Reporting Act, a copy of the report and a summary of your rights under the Fair Credit Reporting Act will be provided as well as any other documents required by law.

2-09 Performance Evaluation

Supervisors and employees are strongly encouraged to discuss job performance and goals on an informal, day-to-day basis. A formal written performance evaluation will be conducted following an employee's introductory period. Additional formal performance evaluations are conducted to provide both supervisors and employees the opportunity to discuss job tasks, identify and correct weaknesses, encourage and recognize strengths, and discuss positive, purposeful approaches for meeting goals.

2-10 Job Descriptions

(YOUR COMPANY NAME) maintains job descriptions to aid in orienting new employees to their jobs, identifying the requirements of each position, establishing hiring criteria, setting standards for employee performance evaluations, and establishing a basis for making reasonable accommodations for individuals with disabilities.

The Human Resources Department and the hiring manager prepare job descriptions when new positions are created. Existing job descriptions are also reviewed and revised in order to ensure that they are up to date. Job descriptions may also be rewritten periodically to reflect any changes in position duties and responsibilities. All employees will be expected to help ensure that their job descriptions are accurate and current, reflecting the work being done.

Employees should remember that job descriptions do not necessarily cover every task or duty that might be assigned, and that additional responsibilities may be assigned as necessary. Contact the Human Resources Department if you have any questions or concerns about your job description.

3-01 Employee Benefits

Eligible employees at (YOUR COMPANY NAME) are provided a wide range of benefits. A number of the programs (such as Social Security, workers' compensation, state disability, and unemployment insurance) cover all employees in the manner prescribed by law.

Benefits eligibility is dependent upon a variety of factors, including employee classification. Your supervisor can identify the programs for which you are eligible. Details of many of these programs can be found elsewhere in the Handbook.

The following benefit programs are available to eligible employees:

- Auto mileage
- Bereavement leave
- Dental insurance
- Holidays
- Medical insurance
- Stock options
- Vacation benefits

Some benefit programs require contributions from the employee, but most are fully paid by (YOUR COMPANY NAME). Many benefits are described in separate Summary Plan Descriptions, or Plans, which may change from time to time. The Summary Plan Description will have control over any policy in this Handbook. You will receive a copy of each Summary Plan Description applicable to you. Contact the Human Resources Department if you need a Summary Plan Description or have any questions.

3-03 Vacation Benefits

Vacation time off with pay is available to eligible employees to provide opportunities for rest, relaxation, and personal pursuits. Employees in the following employment classification(s) are eligible to earn and use vacation time as described in this policy:

Regular full-time employees

The amount of paid vacation time employees receive each year increases with the length of their employment, as shown in the following schedule:

- Upon initial eligibility, the employee is entitled to 10 vacation days each year, accrued monthly at the rate of 0.833 days.
- After four years of eligible service, the employee is entitled to 15 vacation days each year, accrued monthly at the rate of 1.250 days.

The length of eligible service is calculated on the basis of a "benefit year." This is the 12-month period that begins when the employee starts to earn vacation time. An employee's benefit year may be extended for any significant leave of absence except military leave of absence. Military leave has no effect on this calculation. (See individual leave of absence policies for more information.)

Once employees enter an eligible employment classification, they begin to earn paid vacation time according to the schedule. They can request use of vacation time after it is earned.

Paid vacation time can be used in minimum increments of one day. To take vacation, employees should request advance approval from their supervisors. Requests will be reviewed based on a number of factors, including business needs and staffing requirements.

Vacation time off is paid at the employee's base pay rate at the time of vacation. It does not include overtime or any special forms of compensation such as incentives, commissions, bonuses, or shift differentials.

As stated above, employees are encouraged to use available paid vacation time for rest, relaxation, and personal pursuits. In the event that available vacation is not used by the end of the benefit year, employees may carry unused time forward to the next benefit year. If the total amount of unused vacation time reaches a "cap" equal to two times the annual vacation amount, further vacation accrual will stop. When the employee uses paid vacation time and brings the available amount below the cap, vacation accrual will begin again.

Upon termination of employment, employees will be paid for unused vacation time that has been earned through the last day of work.

3-05 Holidays

(YOUR COMPANY NAME) will grant holiday time off to all employees on the holidays listed below:

- New Year's Day (January 1)
- Martin Luther King, Jr. Day (third Monday in January)
- Presidents' Day (third Monday in February)
- Memorial Day (last Monday in May)
- Independence Day (July 4)
- Labor Day (first Monday in September)
- Thanksgiving (fourth Thursday in November)
- Christmas (December 25)
- New Year's Eve (December 31)

(YOUR COMPANY NAME) will grant paid holiday time off to all eligible employees immediately upon assignment to an eligible employment classification. Holiday pay will be calculated based on the employee's straight-time pay rate (as of the date of the holiday) times the number of hours the employee would otherwise have worked on that day. Eligible employee classification(s):

Regular full-time employees

If a recognized holiday falls during an eligible employee's paid absence (e.g., vacation, sick leave), the employee will be ineligible for holiday pay. If eligible nonexempt employees work on a recognized holiday, they will receive holiday pay plus wages at their straight-time rate for the hours worked on the holiday. In addition to the recognized holidays previously listed, eligible employees will receive two floating holidays in each anniversary year. To be eligible, employees must complete three calendar days of service in an eligible employment classification. These holidays must be scheduled with the prior approval of the employee's supervisor.

Paid time off for holidays will be counted as hours worked for the purposes of determining whether overtime pay is owed.

3-06 Workers' Compensation Insurance

(YOUR COMPANY NAME) provides a comprehensive workers' compensation insurance program at no cost to employees, pursuant to law. This program covers any injury or illness sustained in the course of employment that requires medical, surgical, or hospital treatment. Subject to applicable legal requirements, workers' compensation insurance provides benefits after a short waiting period or, if the employee is hospitalized, immediately.

Employees who sustain work-related injuries or illnesses should inform their supervisor immediately. No matter how minor an on-the-job injury may appear, it is important that it be reported immediately. This will enable an eligible employee to qualify for coverage as quickly as possible.

3-07 Sick Leave Benefits

(YOUR COMPANY NAME) provides paid sick leave benefits to all eligible employees for periods of temporary absence due to illnesses or injuries. Eligible employee classification(s):

Regular full-time employees

Eligible employees will accrue sick leave benefits at the rate of 10 days per year (.83 of a day for every full month of service). Sick leave benefits are calculated on the basis of a "benefit year," the 12-month period that begins when the employee starts to earn sick leave benefits.

Paid sick leave can be used in minimum increments of one day. An eligible employee may use sick leave benefits for an absence due to his or her own illness or injury, or that of a child, parent, or spouse of the employee.

Employees who are unable to report to work due to illness or injury should notify their direct supervisor before the scheduled start of their workday if possible. The direct supervisor must also be contacted on each additional day of absence. If an employee is absent for three or more consecutive days due to illness or injury, (YOUR COMPANY NAME) may require a physician's statement verifying the illness or injury and its beginning and expected ending dates. Such verification may be requested for other sick leave absences as well and may be required as a condition to receiving sick leave benefits.

Sick leave benefits will be calculated based on the employee's base pay rate at the time of absence and will not include any special forms of compensation, such as incentives, commissions, bonuses, or shift differentials.

Sick leave benefits are intended solely to provide income protection in the event of illness or injury, and may not be used for any other absence. Unused sick leave benefits will not be paid to employees while they are employed or upon termination of employment.

3-08 Time Off to Vote

(YOUR COMPANY NAME) encourages employees to fulfill their civic responsibilities by participating in elections. Generally, employees are able to find time to vote either before or after their regular work schedule. If employees are unable to vote in an election during their nonworking hours, (YOUR COMPANY NAME) will grant up to two hours of paid time off to vote.

Employees should request time off to vote from their supervisor at least two working days prior to the Election Day. Advance notice is required so that the necessary time off can be scheduled at the beginning or end of the work shift, whichever causes less disruption to the normal work schedule.

Employees must submit a voter's receipt on the first working day following the election to qualify for paid time off.

3-09 Bereavement Leave

Employees who wish to take time off due to the death of an immediate family member should notify their supervisor immediately.

Up to three days of paid bereavement leave will be provided to eligible employees in the following classification(s):

Regular full-time employees

Bereavement pay is calculated based on the base pay rate at the time of absence and will not include any special forms of compensation, such as incentives, commissions, bonuses, or shift differentials.

Bereavement leave will normally be granted unless there are unusual business needs or staffing requirements. Employees may, with their supervisors' approval, use any available paid leave for additional time off as necessary.

(YOUR COMPANY NAME) defines "immediate family" as the employee's spouse, parent, child, or sibling.

3-11 Jury Duty

(YOUR COMPANY NAME) encourages employees to fulfill their civic responsibilities by serving jury duty when required. Employees may request unpaid jury duty leave for the length of absence. If desired, employees may use any available paid time off (for example, vacation benefits).

Employees must show the jury duty summons to their supervisor as soon as possible so that the supervisor may make arrangements to accommodate their absence. Of course, employees are expected to report for work whenever the court schedule permits.

Either (YOUR COMPANY NAME) or the employee may request an excuse from jury duty if, in (YOUR COMPANY NAME) 's judgment, the employee's absence would create serious operational difficulties.

(YOUR COMPANY NAME) will continue to provide health insurance benefits for the full term of the jury duty absence.

Vacation, sick leave, and holiday benefits will continue to accrue during unpaid jury duty leave.

3-13 Benefits Continuation (COBRA)

The federal Consolidated Omnibus Budget Reconciliation Act (COBRA) gives employees and their qualified beneficiaries the opportunity to continue health insurance coverage under (YOUR COMPANY NAME) 's health plan when a "qualifying event" would normally result in the loss of eligibility. Some common qualifying events are resignation, termination of employment, or death of an employee; a reduction in an employee's hours or a leave of absence; an employee's divorce or legal separation; and dependent child no longer meeting eligibility requirements.

Under COBRA, the employee or beneficiary pays the full cost of coverage at (YOUR COMPANY NAME) 's group rates plus an administration fee. (YOUR COMPANY NAME) provides each eligible employee with a written notice describing rights granted under COBRA when the employee becomes eligible for coverage under (YOUR COMPANY NAME) 's health insurance plan. The notice contains important information about the employee's rights and obligations. Contact the Human Resources Department for more information about COBRA.

3-16 Health Insurance

(YOUR COMPANY NAME) 'S health insurance plan provides employees access to medical and dental insurance benefits. Employees in the following employment classification(s) are eligible to participate in the health insurance plan:

Regular full-time employees

Eligible employees may participate in the health insurance plan subject to all terms and conditions of the agreement between (YOUR COMPANY NAME) and the insurance carrier.

A change in employment classification that would result in loss of eligibility to participate in the health insurance plan may qualify an employee for benefits continuation under the Consolidated Omnibus Budget Reconciliation Act (COBRA). Refer to the "Benefits Continuation (COBRA)" policy section 3-13 for more information.

Details of the health insurance plan are described in the Summary Plan Description (SPD). An SPD and information on cost of coverage will be provided in advance of enrollment to eligible employees. Contact the Human Resources Department for more information about health insurance benefits.

4-03 Paydays

All employees are paid monthly on the first day of the month. Each paycheck will include earnings for all work performed through the end of the previous payroll period.

In the event that a regularly scheduled payday falls on a day off, such as a weekend or holiday, employees will receive pay on the last day of work before the regularly scheduled payday.

If a regular payday falls during an employee's vacation, the employee may receive his or her earned wages before departing for vacation if a written request is submitted at least one week prior to departing for vacation.

4-05 Employment Termination

We at (YOUR COMPANY NAME) HAVE THE RIGHT TO FIRE YOU AT WILL!

If there is any stealing, or theft what so ever you will be fire immediately and persecuted to the fullest extent of the law.

Termination of employment is an inevitable part of personnel activity within any organization and many of the reasons for termination are routine. Below are examples of some of the most common circumstances under which employment is terminated:

• Resignation—voluntary employment termination initiated by an employee.
• Discharge—involuntary employment termination initiated by the organization.
• Layoff—involuntary employment termination initiated by the organization because of an organizational change.
• Retirement—voluntary employment termination initiated by the employee meeting age, length of service, and any other criteria for retirement from the organization.

(YOUR COMPANY NAME) will generally schedule exit interviews at the time of employment termination. The exit interview will afford an opportunity to discuss such issues as employee benefits, conversion privileges, repayment of outstanding debts to (YOUR COMPANY NAME), or return of (YOUR COMPANY NAME) -owned property. Suggestions, complaints, and questions can also be voiced.

Nothing in this policy is intended to change the (YOUR COMPANY NAME) 's at-will employment policy. Since employment with (YOUR COMPANY NAME) is based on mutual consent, both the employee and (YOUR COMPANY NAME) have the right to terminate employment at will, with or without cause, at any time. Employees will receive their final pay in accordance with applicable state law.

Employee benefits will be affected by employment termination in the following manner. All accrued, vested benefits that are due and payable at termination will be paid. Some benefits may be continued at the employee's expense if the employee so chooses. The employee will be notified in writing of the benefits that may be continued and of the terms, conditions, and limitations of such continuance. See the "Benefits Continuation (COBRA)" policy section 3-13.

4-09 Administrative Pay Corrections

(YOUR COMPANY NAME) takes all reasonable steps to ensure that employees receive the correct amount of pay in each paycheck and that employees are paid promptly on the scheduled payday.

In the unlikely event that there is an error in the amount of pay, the employee should promptly bring the discrepancy to the attention of the Human Resources Department so that corrections can be made as quickly as possible.

4-10 Pay Deductions and Setoffs

The law requires that (YOUR COMPANY NAME) make certain deductions from every employee's compensation. Among these are applicable federal, state, and local income taxes. (YOUR COMPANY NAME) also must deduct Social Security taxes on each employee's earnings up to a specified limit that is called the Social Security "wage base." (YOUR COMPANY NAME) matches the amount of Social Security taxes paid by each employee.

(YOUR COMPANY NAME) offers programs and benefits beyond those required by law. Eligible employees may voluntarily authorize deductions from their paychecks to cover the costs of participation in these programs. Pay setoffs are pay deductions taken by (YOUR COMPANY NAME), usually to help pay off a debt or obligation to (YOUR COMPANY NAME) or others. If you have questions concerning why deductions were made from your paycheck or how they were calculated, the Human Resources Department can assist in having your questions answered.

5-01 Safety

To assist in providing a safe and healthful work environment for employees, customers, and visitors, (YOUR COMPANY NAME) has established a workplace safety program. This program is a top priority for (YOUR COMPANY NAME). The Human Resources Department has responsibility for implementing, administering, monitoring, and evaluating the safety program. Its success depends on the alertness and personal commitment of all.

(YOUR COMPANY NAME) provides information to employees about workplace safety and health issues through regular internal communication channels such as supervisor-employee meetings, bulletin board postings, e-mail, memos, or other written communications.

Some of the best safety improvement ideas come from employees. Those with ideas, concerns, or suggestions for improved safety in the workplace are encouraged to raise them with their supervisor, or with another supervisor or manager, or bring them to the attention of the Human Resources Department. Reports and concerns about workplace safety issues may be made anonymously if the employee wishes. All reports can be made without fear of reprisal.

Each employee is expected to obey safety rules and to exercise caution in all work activities. Employees must immediately report any unsafe condition to the appropriate supervisor. Employees who violate safety standards, who cause hazardous or dangerous situations, or who fail to report or, where appropriate, remedy such situations may be subject to disciplinary action, up to and including termination of employment.

In the case of accidents that result in injury, regardless of how insignificant the injury may appear, employees should immediately notify the Human Resources Department or the appropriate supervisor. Such reports are necessary to comply with laws and initiate insurance and workers' compensation benefits procedures.

5-02 Work Schedules

Work schedules for employees vary throughout our organization. 9:00 a.m.-6:00 p.m. is a standard workday. Supervisors will advise employees of their individual work schedules. Staffing needs and operational demands may necessitate variations in starting and ending times, as well as variations in the total hours that may be scheduled each day and week.

5-04 Use of Phone and Mail Systems

Personal use of the telephone for long-distance and toll calls is not permitted. Employees should practice discretion when making local personal calls and may be required to reimburse (YOUR COMPANY NAME) for any charges resulting from their personal use of the telephone. To ensure effective telephone communications, employees should always use the approved greeting ("Good Morning, (YOUR COMPANY NAME) " or "Good Afternoon, (YOUR COMPANY NAME)," as applicable) and speak in a courteous and professional manner. Please confirm information received from the caller and hang up only after the caller has done so.

The mail system is reserved for business purposes only. Employees should refrain from sending or receiving personal mail at the workplace. The e-mail system is the property of (YOUR COMPANY NAME). Occasional use of the e-mail system for personal messages is permitted, within reasonable limits. (YOUR COMPANY NAME) will not guarantee the privacy of the e-mail system except to the extent required by law.

5-05 Smoking

Smoking is prohibited throughout the workplace, as required by law. This policy applies equally to all employees, customers, and visitors.

5-06 Rest and Meal Periods

All employees are provided with one one-hour meal period each workday. Supervisors will schedule meal periods to accommodate operating requirements. Employees will be relieved of all active responsibilities and restrictions during meal periods and will not be compensated for that time. Brief rest periods will be allowed, as required by California law.

5-10 Emergency Closings

At times, emergencies such as severe weather, fires, power failures, or earthquakes can disrupt (YOUR COMPANY NAME) operations. In extreme cases, these circumstances may require the closing of a work facility.

In cases where an emergency closing is not authorized, employees who fail to report for work will not be paid for the time off. Employees may request available paid leave time such as unused vacation benefits.

5-12 Business Travel Expenses

(YOUR COMPANY NAME) will reimburse employees for reasonable business travel expenses incurred while on assignments away from the normal work location. The President must approve all business travel in advance. Employees whose travel plans have been approved should make all travel arrangements through (YOUR COMPANY NAME) 's designated travel agency.

When approved, the actual costs of travel, meals, lodging, and other expenses directly related to accomplishing business travel objectives will be reimbursed by (YOUR COMPANY NAME). Employees are expected to limit expenses to reasonable amounts.

Expenses that generally will be reimbursed include the following:

- Airfare or train fare for travel in coach or economy class or the lowest available fare
- Car rental fees, only for compact or mid-sized cars
- Fares for shuttle or airport bus service, where available; costs of public transportation for other ground travel
- Taxi fares, only when there is no less expensive alternative
- Mileage costs for use of personal cars, only when less expensive transportation is not available
- Cost of standard accommodations in low- to mid-priced hotels, motels, or similar lodgings
- Cost of meals, no more than $30.00 a day
- Tips not exceeding 15% of the total cost of a meal or 10% of a taxi fare

- Charges for telephone calls, fax, and similar services required for business purposes

Employees who are involved in an accident while traveling on business must promptly report the incident to their immediate supervisor. Vehicles owned, leased, or rented by ___(YOUR COMPANY NAME) may not be used for personal use without prior approval. When travel is completed, employees should submit completed travel expense reports within 30 days. Reports should be accompanied by receipts for all individual expenses. Employees should contact their supervisor for guidance and assistance on procedures related to travel arrangements, expense reports, reimbursement for specific expenses, or any other business travel issues. Abuse of this business travel expenses policy, including falsifying expense reports to reflect costs not incurred by the employee, can be grounds for disciplinary action, up to and including termination of employment.

5-14 Visitors in the Workplace

To provide for the safety and security of employees and the facilities at (YOUR COMPANY NAME), only authorized visitors are allowed in the workplace. Restricting unauthorized visitors helps maintain safety standards, protects against theft, ensures security of equipment, protects confidential information, safeguards employee welfare, and avoids potential distractions and disturbances. All visitors should enter (YOUR COMPANY NAME) at the main entrance. Authorized visitors will receive directions or be escorted to their destination. Employees are responsible for the conduct and safety of their visitors. If an unauthorized individual is observed on (YOUR COMPANY NAME) 's premises, employees should immediately notify their supervisor or, if necessary, direct the individual to the main entrance.

5-16 Computer and E-mail Usage

Computers, computer files, the e-mail system, and software furnished to employees are (YOUR COMPANY NAME) property intended for business use. Employees should not use a password, access a file, or retrieve any stored communication without authorization.

(YOUR COMPANY NAME) strives to maintain a workplace free of harassment and is sensitive to the diversity of its employees. Therefore, (YOUR COMPANY NAME) prohibits the use of computers and the e-mail system in ways that are disruptive, offensive to others, or harmful to morale.

For example, the display or transmission of sexually explicit images, messages, and cartoons is not allowed. Other such misuse includes, but is not limited to, ethnic slurs, racial comments, off-color jokes, or anything that may be construed as harassment or showing disrespect for others. Employees should notify their immediate supervisor, the Human Resources Department, or any member of management upon learning of violations of this policy. Employees who violate this policy will be subject to disciplinary action, up to and including termination of employment.

5-17 Internet Usage

Internet access to global electronic information resources on the World Wide Web is provided by (YOUR COMPANY NAME) to assist employees in obtaining work-related data and technology. The following guidelines have been established to help ensure responsible and productive Internet usage. While Internet usage is intended for job-related activities, incidental and occasional brief personal use of e-mail and the Internet is permitted within reasonable limits.

All Internet data that is composed, transmitted, or received via our computer communications systems is considered to be part of the official records of (YOUR COMPANY NAME) and, as such, is subject to disclosure to law enforcement or other third parties. Employees should expect only the level of privacy that is warranted by existing law and no more. Consequently, employees should always ensure that the business information contained in Internet e-mail messages and other transmissions is accurate, appropriate, ethical, and lawful. Any questions regarding the legal effect of a message or transmission should be brought to our General Counsel.

Data that is composed, transmitted, accessed, or received via the Internet must not contain content that could be considered discriminatory, offensive, obscene, threatening, harassing, intimidating, or disruptive to any employee or other person. Examples of unacceptable content may include, but are not limited to, sexual comments or images, racial slurs, gender-specific comments, or any other comments or images that could reasonably offend someone on the basis of race, age, sex, religious or political beliefs, national origin, disability, sexual orientation, or any other characteristic protected by law.

The unauthorized use, installation, copying, or distribution of copyrighted, trademarked, or patented material on the Internet is expressly prohibited. As a general rule, if an employee did not create material, does not own the rights to it, or has not gotten authorization for its use, it should not be put on the Internet. Employees are also responsible for ensuring that the person sending any material over the Internet has the appropriate distribution rights. Any questions regarding the use of such information should be brought to our General Counsel.

Internet users should take the necessary anti-virus precautions before downloading or copying any file from the Internet. All downloaded files are to be checked for viruses; all compressed files are to be checked before and after decompression.

Abuse of the Internet access provided by (YOUR COMPANY NAME) in violation of the law or (YOUR COMPANY NAME) policies will result in disciplinary action, up to and including termination of employment. Employees may also be held personally liable for any violations of this policy. The following behaviors are examples of previously stated or additional actions and activities that are prohibited and can result in disciplinary action:

- Sending or posting discriminatory, harassing, or threatening messages or images
- Using the organization's time and resources for personal gain
- Stealing, using, or disclosing someone else's code or password without authorization
- Copying, pirating, or downloading software and electronic files without permission
- Sending or posting confidential material, trade secrets, or proprietary information outside of the organization
- Violating copyright law
- Failing to observe licensing agreements
- Engaging in unauthorized transactions that may incur a cost to the organization or initiate unwanted Internet services and transmissions
- Sending or posting messages or material that could damage the organization's image or reputation
- Participating in the viewing or exchange of pornography or obscene materials
- Sending or posting messages that defame or slander other individuals
- Attempting to break into the computer system of another organization or person
- Refusing to cooperate with a security investigation
- Sending or posting chain letters, solicitations, or advertisements not related to business purposes or activities
- Using the Internet for political causes or activities, religious activities, or any sort of gambling
- Jeopardizing the security of the organization's electronic communications systems
- Sending or posting messages that disparage another organization's products or services
- Passing off personal views as representing those of the organization
- Sending anonymous e-mail messages
- Engaging in any other illegal activities

5-22 Workplace Violence Prevention

(YOUR COMPANY NAME) is committed to preventing workplace violence and to maintaining a safe work environment. Given the increasing violence in society in general, (YOUR COMPANY NAME) has adopted the following guidelines to deal with intimidation, harassment, or other threats of (or actual) violence that may occur during business hours or on its premises.

All employees, including supervisors and temporary employees, should be treated with courtesy and respect at all times. Employees are expected to refrain from fighting, "horseplay," or other conduct that may be dangerous to others. Firearms, weapons, and other dangerous or hazardous devices or substances are prohibited from the premises of (YOUR COMPANY NAME) without proper authorization.

Conduct that threatens, intimidates, or coerces another employee, a customer, or a member of the public at any time, including off-duty periods, will not be tolerated. This prohibition includes all acts of harassment, including harassment that is based on an individual's sex, race, age, or any characteristic protected by federal, state, or local law.

All threats of (or actual) violence, both direct and indirect, should be reported as soon as possible to your immediate supervisor or any other member of management. This includes threats by employees, as well as threats by customers, vendors, solicitors, or other members of the public. When reporting a threat of violence, you should be as specific and detailed as possible.

All suspicious individuals or activities should also be reported as soon as possible to a supervisor. Do not place yourself in peril. If you see or hear a commotion or disturbance near your workstation, do not try to intercede or see what is happening. (YOUR COMPANY NAME) will promptly and thoroughly investigate all reports of threats of (or actual) violence and of suspicious individuals or activities. The identity of the individual making a report will be protected as much as is practical.

Anyone determined to be responsible for threats of (or actual) violence or other conduct that is in violation of these guidelines will be subject to prompt disciplinary action, up to and including termination of employment.

(YOUR COMPANY NAME) encourages employees to bring their disputes or differences with other employees to the attention of their supervisors or the Human Resources Department before the situation escalates into potential violence. (YOUR COMPANY NAME) is eager to assist in the resolution of employee disputes and will not discipline employees for raising such concerns.

6-01 Medical Leave

(YOUR COMPANY NAME) provides medical leaves of absence without pay to eligible employees who are temporarily unable to work due to a serious health condition or disability. For purposes of this policy, serious health conditions or disabilities include inpatient care in a hospital, hospice, or residential medical care facility and continuing treatment by a health care provider.

Employees in the following employment classifications are eligible to request medical leave as described in this policy:

Regular full-time employees

Eligible employees should make requests for medical leave to their supervisors at least 30 days in advance of foreseeable events and as soon as possible for unforeseeable events.

A health care provider's statement must be submitted verifying the need for medical leave and its beginning and expected ending dates. Any changes in this information should be promptly reported to (YOUR COMPANY NAME). Employees returning from medical leave must submit a health care provider's verification of their fitness to return to work.

Eligible employees are normally granted leave for the period of the disability, up to a maximum of 12 weeks within any 12-month period. Any combination of medical leave and family leave may not exceed this maximum limit. If the initial period of approved absence proves insufficient, consideration will be given to a request for an extension.

Employees who sustain work-related injuries are eligible for a medical leave of absence for the period of the disability, in accordance with all applicable laws covering occupational disabilities.

Subject to the terms, conditions, and limitations of the applicable plans, (YOUR COMPANY NAME) will continue to provide health insurance benefits for the full period of the approved medical leave.

Benefit accruals, such as vacation, sick leave, and holiday benefits, will continue during the approved medical leave period.

So that an employee's return to work can be properly scheduled, an employee on medical leave is requested to provide (YOUR COMPANY NAME) with at least two weeks' advance notice of the date the employee intends to return to work. When a medical leave ends, the employee will be reinstated to the same position, if it is available, or to an equivalent position for which the employee is qualified.

If an employee fails to return to work on the agreed-upon return date, (YOUR COMPANY NAME) will assume that the employee has resigned.

6-02 Family Leave

(YOUR COMPANY NAME) provides family leaves of absence without pay to eligible employees who wish to take time off from work duties to fulfill family obligations relating directly to childbirth, adoption, or placement of a foster child or to care for a child, spouse, or parent with a serious health condition. A "serious health condition" means an illness, injury, impairment, or physical or mental condition that involves inpatient care in a hospital, hospice, or residential medical care facility or continuing treatment by a health care provider.

Employees in the following employment classifications are eligible to request family leave as described in this policy:

Regular full-time employees

Eligible employees should make requests for family leave to their supervisors at least 30 days in advance of foreseeable events and as soon as possible for unforeseeable events. Employees requesting family leave related to the serious health condition of a child, spouse, or parent may be required to submit a health care provider's statement verifying the need for family leave to provide care, its beginning and expected ending dates, and the estimated time required.

Eligible employees may request up to a maximum of 12 weeks of family leave within any 12-month period. Any combination of family leave and medical leave may not exceed this maximum. Married employee couples may be restricted to a combined total of 12 weeks leave within any 12-month period for childbirth, adoption, or placement of a foster child or to care for a parent with a serious health condition.

Subject to the terms, conditions, and limitations of the applicable plans, (YOUR COMPANY NAME) will continue to provide health insurance benefits for the full period of the approved family leave. Benefit accruals, such as vacation, sick leave, and holiday benefits, will continue during the approved family leave period.

So that an employee's return to work can be properly scheduled, an employee on family leave is requested to provide (YOUR COMPANY NAME) with at least two weeks' advance notice of the date the employee intends to return to work. When families leave ends, the employee will be reinstated to the same position, if it is available, or to an equivalent position for which the employee is qualified. If an employee fails to return to work on the agreed-upon return date, (YOUR COMPANY NAME) will assume that the employee has resigned.

6-07 Pregnancy Disability Leave

(YOUR COMPANY NAME) provides pregnancy disability leaves of absence without pay to eligible employees who are temporarily unable to work due to a disability related to pregnancy, childbirth, or related medical conditions. Any employee is eligible to request pregnancy disability leave as described in this policy. Employees should make requests for pregnancy disability leave to their supervisors at least 30 days in advance of foreseeable events and as soon as possible for unforeseeable events. A health care provider's statement must be submitted verifying the need for pregnancy disability leave and its beginning and expected ending dates. Any changes in this information should be promptly reported to (YOUR COMPANY NAME). Employees returning from pregnancy disability leave must submit a health care provider's verification of their fitness to return to work.

Employees are normally granted unpaid leave for the period of the disability, up to a maximum of four months. Employees may substitute any accrued paid leave time for unpaid leave as part of the pregnancy disability leave period. Subject to the terms, conditions, and limitations of the applicable plans, (YOUR COMPANY NAME) will continue to provide health insurance benefits for the full period of the approved pregnancy disability leave. So that an employee's return to work can be properly scheduled, an employee on pregnancy disability leave is requested to provide (YOUR COMPANY NAME) with at least two weeks' advance notice of the date she intends to return to work.

When a pregnancy disability leave ends, the employee will be reinstated to the same position, unless either the employee would not otherwise have been employed for legitimate business reasons or each means of preserving the job would substantially undermine the ability to operate (YOUR COMPANY NAME) safely and efficiently. If the same position is not available, the employee will be offered a comparable position in terms of such issues as pay, location, job content, and promotional opportunities.

If an employee fails to report to work promptly at the end of the pregnancy disability leave, (YOUR COMPANY NAME) will assume that the employee has resigned.

7-01 Employee Conduct and Work Rules

To ensure orderly operations and provide the best possible work environment, (YOUR COMPANY NAME) expects employees to follow rules of conduct that will protect the interests and safety of all employees and the organization.

It is not possible to list all the forms of behavior that are considered unacceptable in the workplace. The following are examples of infractions of rules of conduct that may result in disciplinary action, up to and including termination of employment:

- Theft or inappropriate removal or possession of property
- Falsification of timekeeping records
- Working under the influence of alcohol or illegal drugs
- Possession, distribution, sale, transfer, or use of alcohol or illegal drugs in the workplace, while on duty or while operating employer-owned vehicles or equipment
- Fighting or threatening violence in the workplace
- Boisterous or disruptive activity in the workplace
- Negligence or improper conduct leading to damage of employer-owned or customer-owned property
- Insubordination or other disrespectful conduct
- Violation of safety or health rules
- Smoking in the workplace

- Sexual or other unlawful or unwelcome harassment
- Possession of dangerous or unauthorized materials, such as explosives or firearms, in the workplace
- Excessive absenteeism or any absence without notice
- Unauthorized disclosure of business "secrets" or confidential information
- Violation of personnel policies
- Unsatisfactory performance or conduct

Nothing is this policy is intended to change the (YOUR COMPANY NAME) 's at-will employment policy. Employment with (YOUR COMPANY NAME) is at the mutual consent of (YOUR COMPANY NAME) and the employee, and either party may terminate that relationship at any time, with or without cause, and with or without advance notice.

7-02 Drug and Alcohol Use

It is (YOUR COMPANY NAME) 's desire to provide a drug-free, healthful, and safe workplace. To promote this goal, employees are required to report to work in appropriate mental and physical condition to perform their jobs in a satisfactory manner.

While on (YOUR COMPANY NAME) premises and while conducting business-related activities off (YOUR COMPANY NAME) premises, no employee may use, possess, distribute, sell, or be under the influence of alcohol or illegal drugs. The legal use of prescribed drugs is permitted on the job only if it does not impair an employee's ability to perform the essential functions of the job effectively and in a safe manner that does not endanger other individuals in the workplace.

Violations of this policy may lead to disciplinary action, up to and including immediate termination of employment, and/or required participation in a substance abuse rehabilitation or treatment program. Such violations may also have legal consequences.

Employees with questions or concerns about substance dependency or abuse are encouraged to discuss these matters with their supervisor or the Human Resources Department to receive assistance or referrals to appropriate resources in the community.

Employees with problems with alcohol and certain drugs that have not resulted in, and are not the immediate subject of, disciplinary action may request approval to take unpaid time off to participate in a rehabilitation or treatment program through (YOUR COMPANY NAME) 's health insurance benefit coverage. Leave may be granted if the employee agrees to abstain from use of the problem substance and abides by all (YOUR COMPANY NAME) policies, rules, and prohibitions relating to conduct in the workplace; and if granting the leave will not cause (YOUR COMPANY NAME) any undue hardship.

Employees with questions on this policy or issues related to drug or alcohol use in the workplace should raise their concerns with their supervisor or the Human Resources Department without fear of reprisal.

7-03 Sexual and Other Unlawful Harassment

(YOUR COMPANY NAME) is committed to providing a work environment that is free from all forms of discrimination and conduct that can be considered harassing, coercive, or disruptive, including sexual harassment. Actions, words, jokes, or comments based on an individual's sex, race, color, national origin, age, religion, disability, sexual orientation, or any other legally protected characteristic will not be tolerated.

Sexual harassment is defined as unwanted sexual advances, or visual, verbal, or physical conduct of a sexual nature. This definition includes many forms of offensive behavior and includes gender-based harassment of a person of the same sex as the harasser. The following is a partial list of sexual harassment examples:

• Unwanted sexual advances
• Offering employment benefits in exchange for sexual favors
• Making or threatening reprisals after a negative response to sexual advances
• Visual conduct that includes leering, making sexual gestures, or displaying of sexually suggestive objects or pictures, cartoons, or posters
• Verbal conduct that includes making or using derogatory comments, epithets, slurs, or jokes
• Verbal sexual advances or propositions
• Verbal abuse of a sexual nature, graphic verbal commentaries about an individual's body, sexually degrading words used to describe an individual, or suggestive or obscene letters, notes, or invitations
• Physical conduct that includes touching, assaulting, or impeding or blocking movements

Unwelcome sexual advances (either verbal or physical), requests for sexual favors, and other verbal or physical conduct of a sexual nature constitute sexual harassment when: (1) submission to such conduct is made either explicitly or implicitly a term or condition of employment; (2) submission to or rejection of the conduct is used as a basis for making employment decisions; or (3) the conduct has the purpose or effect of interfering with work performance or creating an intimidating, hostile, or offensive work environment.

If you experience or witness sexual or other unlawful harassment in the workplace, report it immediately to your supervisor. If the supervisor is unavailable or you believe it would be inappropriate to contact that person, you should immediately contact the Human Resources Department or any other member of management. You can raise concerns and make reports without fear of reprisal or retaliation.

All allegations of sexual harassment will be quickly and discreetly investigated. To the extent possible, your confidentiality and that of any witnesses and the alleged harasser will be protected against unnecessary disclosure. When the investigation is completed, you will be informed of the outcome of the investigation.

Any supervisor or manager who becomes aware of possible sexual or other unlawful harassment must immediately advise the Human Resources Department or the President of the (YOUR COMPANY NAME) so it can be investigated in a timely and confidential manner. Anyone engaging in sexual or other unlawful behavior will be subject to disciplinary action, up to and including termination of employment.

7-04 Attendance and Punctuality

To maintain a safe and productive work environment, (YOUR COMPANY NAME) expects employees to be reliable and to be punctual in reporting for scheduled work. Absenteeism and tardiness place a burden on other employees and on (YOUR COMPANY NAME). In the rare instances when employees cannot avoid being late to work or are unable to work as scheduled, they should notify their supervisor or the Human Resources Department as soon as possible in advance of the anticipated tardiness or absence.

Poor attendance and excessive tardiness are disruptive. Either may lead to disciplinary action, up to and including termination of employment.

7-05 Personal Appearance

Dress, grooming, and personal cleanliness standards contribute to the morale of all employees and affect the business image that (YOUR COMPANY NAME) presents to the community.

During business hours or when representing (YOUR COMPANY NAME), you are expected to present a clean, neat, and tasteful appearance. You should dress and groom yourself according to the requirements of your position and accepted social standards.

Your supervisor or department head is responsible for establishing a reasonable dress code appropriate to the job you perform. If your supervisor feels that your personal appearance is inappropriate, you may be asked to leave the workplace until you are properly dressed or groomed. Under such circumstances, you will not be compensated for the time away from work. Consult your supervisor if you have questions as to what constitutes appropriate appearance. Where necessary, reasonable accommodation may be made to a person with a disability.

7-06 Return of Property

Employees are responsible for all (YOUR COMPANY NAME) property, materials, or written information issued to them or in their possession or control. Employees must return all (YOUR COMPANY NAME) property immediately upon request or upon termination of employment. Where permitted by applicable laws, (YOUR COMPANY NAME) may withhold from the employee's check or final paycheck the cost of any items that are not returned when required. (YOUR COMPANY NAME) may also take all action deemed appropriate to recover or protect its property.

7-08 Resignation

Resignation is a voluntary act initiated by the employee to terminate employment with (YOUR COMPANY NAME). Although advance notice is not required, (YOUR COMPANY NAME) requests at least two weeks' written notice of resignation from nonexempt employees and two weeks' written notice of resignation from exempt employees.

Prior to an employee's departure, an exit interview will be scheduled to discuss the reasons for resignation and the effect of the resignation on benefits.

7-10 Security Inspections

(YOUR COMPANY NAME) wishes to maintain a work environment that is free of illegal drugs, alcohol, firearms, explosives, or other improper materials. To this end, (YOUR COMPANY NAME) prohibits the possession, transfer, sale, or use of such materials on its premises. (YOUR COMPANY NAME) requires the cooperation of all employees in administering this policy.

Desks, lockers, and other storage devices may be provided for the convenience of employees but remains the sole property of (YOUR COMPANY NAME). Accordingly, they, as well as any articles found within them, can be inspected by any agent or representative of (YOUR COMPANY NAME) at any time, either with or without prior notice.

7-12 Solicitation

In an effort to ensure a productive and harmonious work environment, persons not employed by (YOUR COMPANY NAME) may not solicit or distribute literature in the workplace at any time for any purpose.

(YOUR COMPANY NAME) recognizes that employees may have interests in events and organizations outside the workplace. However, employees may not solicit or distribute literature concerning these activities during working time. (Working time does not include lunch periods, work breaks, or any other periods in which employees are not on duty.)

Examples of impermissible forms of solicitation include:

- The collection of money, goods, or gifts for community groups
- The collection of money, goods, or gifts for religious groups
- The collection of money, goods, or gifts for political groups
- The collection of money, goods, or gifts for charitable groups
- The sale of goods, services, or subscriptions outside the scope of official organization business
- The circulation of petitions
- The distribution of literature in working areas at any time
- The solicitation of memberships, fees, or dues
  In addition, the posting of written solicitations on (YOUR COMPANY NAME) bulletin boards and solicitations by e-mail are restricted. (YOUR COMPANY NAME) bulletin boards display important information; employees should consult them frequently for:
- Affirmative Action statement
- Employee announcements
- Workers' compensation insurance information
- State disability insurance/unemployment insurance information
  If employees have a message of interest to the workplace, they may submit it to the Human Resources Director for approval. The Human Resources Director will post all approved messages.

7-16 Progressive Discipline

The purpose of this policy is to state (YOUR COMPANY NAME) 's position on administering equitable and consistent discipline for unsatisfactory conduct in the workplace. The best disciplinary measure is the one that does not have to be enforced and comes from good leadership and fair supervision at all employment levels.

(YOUR COMPANY NAME) 's own best interest lies in ensuring fair treatment of all employees and in making certain that disciplinary actions are prompt, uniform, and impartial. The major purpose of any disciplinary action is to correct the problem, prevent recurrence, and prepare the employee for satisfactory service in the future.

Although employment with (YOUR COMPANY NAME) is based on mutual consent and both the employee and (YOUR COMPANY NAME) have the right to terminate employment at will, with or without cause or advance notice, (YOUR COMPANY NAME) may use progressive discipline at its discretion.

Disciplinary action may call for any of four steps—verbal warning, written warning, suspension with or without pay, or termination of employment— depending on the severity of the problem and the number of occurrences.

Progressive discipline means that, with respect to many disciplinary problems, these four steps will normally be followed. However, there may be circumstances when one or more steps are bypassed.

(YOUR COMPANY NAME) recognizes that there are certain types of employee problems that are serious enough to justify either a suspension or, in extreme situations, termination of employment, without going through the usual progressive discipline steps.

While it is impossible to list every type of behavior that may be deemed a serious offense, the Employee Conduct and Work Rules policy includes examples of problems that may result in immediate suspension or termination of employment. However, the problems listed are not all necessarily serious offenses, but may be examples of unsatisfactory conduct that will trigger progressive discipline.

By using progressive discipline, we hope that most employee problems can be corrected at an early stage, benefiting both the employee and (YOUR COMPANY NAME).

7-18 Problem Resolution

(YOUR COMPANY NAME) is committed to providing the best possible working conditions for its employees. Part of this commitment is encouraging an open and frank atmosphere in which any problem, complaint, suggestion, or question receives a timely response from (YOUR COMPANY NAME) supervisors and management.

(YOUR COMPANY NAME) strives to ensure fair and honest treatment of all employees. Supervisors, managers, and employees are expected to treat each other with respect. Employees are encouraged to offer positive and constructive criticism.

If employees disagree with established rules of conduct, policies, or practices, they can express their concern through the problem resolution procedure. No employee will be penalized, formally or informally, for voicing a complaint with (YOUR COMPANY NAME) in a reasonable, business-like manner, or for using the problem resolution procedure.

If a situation occurs when employees believe that a condition of employment or a decision affecting them is unjust or inequitable, they are encouraged to make use of the following steps. The employee may discontinue the procedure at any step.

1. The employee presents the problem to his or her immediate supervisor after the incident occurs. If the supervisor is unavailable or the employee believes it would be inappropriate to contact that person, the employee may present the

problem to the Human Resources Department or the CEO.

2. The supervisor responds to the problem during discussion or after consulting with appropriate management, when necessary. The supervisor documents this discussion.

3. The employee presents the problem to the Human Resources Department if the problem is unresolved.

4. The Human Resources Department counsels and advises the employee, assists in putting the problem in writing, and visits with the employee's manager(s).

Not every problem can be resolved to everyone's total satisfaction, but only through understanding and discussing mutual problems can employees and management develop confidence in each other. This confidence is important to the operation of an efficient and harmonious work environment.

8-00 Life-Threatening Illnesses in the Workplace

Employees with life-threatening illnesses, such as cancer, heart disease, and AIDS, often wish to continue their normal pursuits, including work, to the extent allowed by their condition. (YOUR COMPANY NAME) supports these endeavors as long as the employees are able to meet acceptable performance standards. As in the case of other disabilities, (YOUR COMPANY NAME) will make reasonable accommodations in accordance with all legal requirements, to allow qualified employees with life-threatening illnesses to perform the essential functions of their jobs.

Medical information on individual employees is treated confidentially. (YOUR COMPANY NAME) will take reasonable precautions to protect such information from inappropriate disclosure. Managers and other employees have a responsibility to respect and maintain the confidentiality of employee medical information. Anyone inappropriately disclosing such information is subject to disciplinary action, up to and including termination of employment.

Employees with questions or concerns about life-threatening illnesses are encouraged to contact the Human Resources Department for information and referral to appropriate services and resources.

8-06 Suggestions

As employees of (YOUR COMPANY NAME), you have the opportunity to contribute to our future success and growth by submitting suggestions for practical work-improvement or cost-savings ideas.

All regular employees are eligible to participate in the suggestion program.

A suggestion is an idea that will benefit (YOUR COMPANY NAME) by solving a problem, reducing costs, improving operations or procedures, enhancing customer service, eliminating waste or spoilage, or making (YOUR COMPANY NAME) a better or safer place to work. All suggestions should contain a description of the problem or condition to be improved, a detailed explanation of the solution or improvement, and the reasons why it should be implemented. Statements of problems without accompanying solutions or recommendations concerning co-workers and management are not appropriate suggestions. If you have questions or need advice about your idea, contact your supervisor for help.

Submit suggestions to the Human Resources Department and, after review, they will be forwarded to the Suggestion Committee. As soon as possible, you will be notified of the adoption or rejection of your suggestion. Special recognition and, optionally, a cash award will be given to employees who submit a suggestion that is implemented.

An example of an "Offer of Employment and Employment Contract":

LOGO HERE

Offer of Employment and Employment Contract

Date

Employee Name _____

Address _____

Dear _____:

We are pleased to offer you a position with (Your Company Name). Your start date_____ manager, compensation, benefits, and other terms of employment will be as set forth below and on EXHIBIT A.

TERMS OF EMPLOYMENT

1. **Position and Duties.** Company shall employ you, and you agree to competently and professionally perform such duties as are customarily the responsibility of the position as set forth in the job description attached as EXHIBIT A, which is also verbally told, and taught to you by a manager or supervisor, and as reasonably assigned to you from time to time by your Manager as set forth in.

2. **Outside Business Activities.** During your employment with Company, you shall devote competent energies, interests, and abilities to the performance of your duties under this Agreement. During the term of this Agreement, you shall not, without Company's prior written consent, render any services to others for compensation or engage or participate, actively or passively, in any other business activities that would interfere with the performance of your duties hereunder or compete with Company's business.

3. **Employment Classification.** You shall be a Full-Time Employee and shall not be entitled to benefits except as specifically outlined herein.

4. **Compensation/Benefits.**

4.1 **Wage.** Company shall pay you the wage as set forth in the job description attached as EXHIBIT A.

4.2 **Reimbursement of Expenses**. You shall be reimbursed for all reasonable and necessary expenses paid or incurred by you in the performance of your duties. You shall provide Company with original receipts for such expenses.

4.3 **Withholdings.** All compensation paid to you under this Agreement, including payment of salary and taxable benefits, shall be subject to such withholdings as may be required by law or Company's general practices.

4.4 **Benefits.** You will also receive Company's standard employee benefits package (including health insurance), and will be subject to Company's vacation policy as such package and policy are in effect from time to time.

5. **At-Will Employment.** Either party may terminate this Agreement by written notice at any time for any reason or for no reason. This Agreement is intended to be and shall be deemed to be an at-will employment Agreement and does not constitute a guarantee of continuing employment for any term.

6. **Nondisclosure Agreement.** You agree to sign Company's standard Employee Nondisclosure Agreement and Proprietary Rights Assignment as a condition of your employment. We wish to impress upon you that we do not wish you to bring with you any confidential or proprietary material of any former employer or to violate any other obligation to your former employers.

7. **Authorization to Work.** Because of federal regulations adopted in the Immigration Reform and Control Act of 1986, you will need to present documentation demonstrating that you have authorization to work in the United States.

8. **Further Assurances.** Each party shall perform any and all further acts and execute and deliver any documents that are reasonably necessary to carry out the intent of this Agreement.

9. **Notices.** All notices or other communications required or permitted by this Agreement or by law shall be in writing and shall be deemed duly served and given when delivered personally or by facsimile, air courier, certified mail (return receipt requested), postage and fees prepaid, to the party at the address indicated in the signature block or at such other address as a party may request in writing.

10. **Governing Law.** This Agreement shall be governed and interpreted in accordance with the laws of the State of California, as such laws are applied to agreements between residents of California to be performed entirely within the State of California.

11. **Entire Agreement.** This Agreement sets forth the entire Agreement between the parties pertaining to the subject matter hereof and supersedes all prior written agreements and all prior or contemporaneous oral Agreements and understandings, expressed or implied.

12. **Written Modification and Waiver.** No modification to this Agreement, nor any waiver of any rights, shall be effective unless assented to in writing by the party to be charged, and the waiver of any breach or default shall not constitute a

waiver of any other right or any subsequent breach or default.

13. **Assignment.** This Agreement is personal in nature, and neither of the parties shall, without the consent of the other, assign or transfer this Agreement or any rights or obligations under this Agreement, except that Company may assign or transfer this Agreement to a successor of Company's business, in the event of the transfer or sale of all or substantially all of the assets of Company's business, or to a subsidiary, provided that in the case of any assignment or transfer under the terms of this Section, this Agreement shall be binding on and inure to the benefit of the successor of Company's business, and the successor of Company's business shall discharge and perform all of the obligations of Company under this Agreement.

14. **Severability.** If any of the provisions of this Agreement are determined to be invalid, illegal, or unenforceable, such provisions shall be modified to the minimum extent necessary to make such provisions enforceable, and the remaining provisions shall continue in full force and effect to the extent the economic benefits conferred upon the parties by this Agreement remain substantially unimpaired.

15. **Arbitration of Disputes.** Any controversy or claim arising out of or relating to this contract, or the breach thereof, shall be settled by arbitration administered by the American Arbitration Association under its National Rules for the Resolution of Employment Disputes, and judgment upon the award rendered by the arbitrator(s) may be entered by any court having jurisdiction thereof.

We look forward to your arrival and what we hope will be the start of a mutually satisfying work relationship.

Sincerely,

(Your Company Name)

By: _____

Acknowledged, Accepted, and Agreed

Date: _____

_____

Employee Signature

"I always wonder why birds stay in the same place when they can fly anywhere on the earth. Then I ask myself the same question."

-Unknown

ABOUT THE AUTHOR

Natischa Harvey is a successful entrepreneur, wife, and mother of four. She obtains a Masters Degree in Business Administration, spearheads several companies, and has several successful businesses, which she has had for over ten years. Mrs. Harvey has been awarded, recognized, nominated, and honored for many prestigious awards recognizing her for her business achievements, success, and accomplishments. She, as well as her work, has also been featured in several magazines. Mrs. Harvey continues to run her business organizations while also providing consulting advice to others in their business start-ups.

www.ingramcontent.com/pod-product-compliance
Lightning Source LLC
Chambersburg PA
CBHW060620210326
41520CB00010B/1404